Dating After 30
It Doesn't Have To
Suck!

JUN   2009

Dating After 30
It Doesn't Have To
Suck!

Blaise C. Hancock

Burnin' Media Publishing, Inc. - New York

Dating After 30 It Doesn't Have To Suck!
By Blaise C. Hancock

Published by Burnin' Media Publishing, NY, NY.

Book cover art: Ian Jobson
Back cover photo: Walter Kurtz

Editing by Brevard N. Hudson

PRINTED IN THE UNITED STATES OF AMERICA

Hancock, Blaise C.
Dating After 30 It Doesn't Have to Suck!
2nd Edition

1. Author 2. Title 3. Personal 4. Relationships
Library of Congress Control Number: 2008906453
ISBN: 978-0-9792989-2-9   Softcover

For all my single friends.

TABLE OF CONTENTS

Chapter 1
Introduction - *What is the Point?*

Dating is not supposed to be hard. Let me say that again: Dating is NOT supposed to be hard. For many people, including me, dating was an unpleasant, constant reminder that at the end of the day, I was going to bed and waking up alone. For anyone reading this book, that is NOT supposed to be the case. Dating is supposed to be fun. So I'm going to take you on a journey of discovery about yourself and what you really want. This is the journey you need to travel in order to leave the bad dating experiences behind. I will be honest, whether it is harsh or not. You have to get out there, even at 65 years old, because you may still have 40 years left – and that is a long time to be alone.

I believe there are spiritual laws that govern who we attract into our lives. I also believe that we have the power to choose who comes into our lives, so we have to choose carefully. Most people go through life without a thought about what choices they have made to bring certain people into their lives. The problem with that behavior is that you can consistently attract the wrong people. You can even go one step worse, attract the right people into your life, but not know they are right, and scare them off with all those wrong people that seem to linger around you. This can even happen to charismatic people and very good-looking people.

It is a healthy and necessary thing to take time out once in a while and clean house thoroughly. I believe we need to do this with our friendships and business relationships as well. Those who are not positive contributors to your life need to be less prominent or eliminated altogether. If you want to be happy in life, each of us must choose consciously to surround ourselves with people who are positive contributors. Be wary of the one who make you laugh at their tragedy. As funny as the jokes may be, the tragedy that is the source, can bring you down. Generally, funny people are always good to have around. Just make sure that the laughter does not come with too high a price. I have a good friend who loves to tell amusing stories about his dating experiences. Unfortunately his stories always end with a down note. This is what you want to avoid. My friend told one story about dating a girl he really liked for several weeks. Then the two arranged to spend a weekend together. They planned to go up to the girl's house in the country for what he expected to be a romantic weekend. He looked forward to the time together, and speculated about where this private time with each other would lead the relationship. He worried about what to pack, whether they would have sex, what to say and do... Then the weekend's romance was cut short. The husband showed up!

While he survived unscathed and this makes for an amusing story, this is only one example. The problem for my friend is that story after story ends in a tragic way. The more stories like this that you hear, the more likely it seems that the person telling them is a tragic case.

On to the dating background: I started dating in high school like most people. When I was in high school, dates were rarely one-on-one and generally involved going somewhere with a group of friends. This group dynamic helped to lighten the pressure, and provided plenty of lively conversation. In later years, this group dynamic would have been a huge help when a date was a total dud and there was no one else to talk to for a few hours.

I have dated all types, all different income levels, ethnicities, various heights, religious backgrounds and nationalities. My brother once said I was like the United Nations of dating (only he wasn't that polite).

What it took me years to realize is that there are three ways of going about meeting the right one. First, there are those who sit around and just wait for the phone to ring. They are the ones who never pursue anyone. They hope their friends will set them up or that someone in the office will ask them out. They also hope that the person next to them in the gym will say something, or at least give some indication of interest. They may go out to bars or clubs with friends, but they rarely look around and they never approach anyone. It's just too risky. What would happen if they were rejected? The thought process of these people is such that they are terrified of any encounter where they might be rejected. If they actually spoke up and were rebuffed, they would simply have to go hide in the bathroom for an hour, until they were sure that the rejecter had left. There is another subset of this take-no-action group, those that believe if it happens, it happens. These folks have a laissez faire attitude and follow a path of non-interference, even when it comes to their own love life. Another subset believes that they are good enough as they are and that anyone who does not approach them is gutless. They expect others to be strong-willed enough to approach, regardless of the attitude or vibe they give off to others.

These folks are very lucky sometimes and just the right person approaches them. If they are fortunate and that person works out, bless them.

I am not one of these folks. As an adolescent I was terrified to talk to strangers. My stepmother was well read and one of the books she bought for me was called: "Stand up, Shake Hands, Say 'How do you Do'."[i] She forced me to play host and make people feel welcome in our home. We often hosted brunch at our home, after church on Sundays. Because I was terribly shy, I was the one assigned to answer the door, invite guests in to the living room and get drink orders from them. As people arrived, I had a very specific task and there is no way to do it without talking to people. It was a subtle way of forcing me out of my shell.

I had to tell whoever was bartending what drink people would like, and then deliver it to them. After my tasks were done, I could retreat. Perhaps that is why brunch is my favorite way of getting together with people as an adult. It is not as serious as dinner. Brunches can be brief or if the conversation is lively, a brunch can go on for hours.

Once I got past the shyness, I took the lead a bit more in terms of meeting people. I was not assaulting anyone, but I was not about to let opportunities pass me by.

However my goal in writing this book is to help you stop CHASING new people and start ATTRACTING them instead.

Second - Plenty of people go out into the world and are like predators, hunting for the next prey. Admittedly, this may be done in a coy and seductive manner, while some are aggressive and almost boastful in their method and appearance. Either way, they are hunters.

Most men learn to pursue women like the tigers in a jungle. Just like the tigers hide in trees and tall grasses, stalking their prey, men lurk in bars hidden but peering through the crowd. When a group of innocent prey wonders by, the tiger waits for the just the right moment and then leaps at his prey. If he does not catch one on the first movement, he chases down his prey as they run from him, just as the single men leap at the first attractive woman who wonders from her pack. The next day the tiger begins the process all over again (just like the single man).

Does this sound familiar to you?

Of course we have all seen the human counterparts to the tiger. We have seen the women in a bar move slowly away, not running, but close to it. Have you been the predator or the prey? Maybe like me, you have been both. Chasing the ones you like and then running from the ones who scare you.

Women too can be predators. I have sat on the side of a children's baseball game and had the divorcees gossip in front of me about which dad is single and has money. Then they each vie for his attention.

Third - Now imagine you are trying to catch bees. Do you run around with a net, chasing down each bee? Or do you put out honey and let the scent attract the bees to you? Would you rather have a few dozen bees or hundreds? Would you rather be expending all your energy as the chaser or predator; or would you rather attract the eligible singles to you like bees to honey?

Your "honey" in this case, is the way you present yourself: physically, mentally and emotionally. The honey is whatever about you that you can use to draw others to you. Your intellect, your sense of humor, your looks, your walk, the way you turn a phrase, any of these things become the "honey" that you use to pull people toward you.

Do not wait around and just end up with whomever bothers to notice you sitting in a corner, because you were totally passive about dating. But you also do not want to be known as the dating predator either. Be the one who follows the third path and draws people to you. Create the best "YOU" that you can be. Then position yourself in the midst of the people who include the type of mate you seek. We will get into more detail in the coming chapters. But the idea is that once you are ready on the inside and on the outside, you must get out and do the things you enjoy. This will attract that special someone to you.

Chapter 2
Internal Feelings

Are you right in the head?

Okay, that is kind of an insult – except it is also a valid question. If your mindset is not right, then you will continually attract the wrong people. If you were to step outside yourself for a moment, how do other people see you? Do they think you look desperate? Do you have a negative attitude? Do you take pride in your appearance? If you brought someone inside your home – even just for a drink or to continue a conversation – would the look of your home scare him off?

You have to conquer your fears to get yourself right, or ready in the head, for dating. Fears will keep you from taking the leaps of faith that you will need to make, to change your life and ready yourself for love. You have to make yourself your own role model. Take risks; create excitement in your life. I am not saying that you should do anything stupid, but if you are 55 years old and you dream of sky diving – go do it before your bones are too brittle for you to jump from the plane!

There is a wonderful Lee Ann Womack country song: *I Hope You Dance,* that says: "If you get the chance to sit it out or dance... dance." This is a motto to live by. If you never have people over because you fear having a terrible party in your home where everything goes wrong – Conquer this fear! You may want to buy ready-to-serve food and download a great play list of songs for background music to ensure that things go well. Conquer the fear and dance! Invite people from your office, from a class you are taking, or other single moms from the sports teams of your children, or even a few members of your church.

Searching for a mate after age 30 must be done from the perspective of what man will mesh with your life, not which one will look hottest on your arm. This means you need to have a better idea of what attributes are most important to you. The person on your arm should not be viewed as a material asset, but as a life contributor.

If you say, "I wanna be married by the time I'm ___ age" then you are setting yourself up for failure. Or you could be setting yourself up for marriage to the WRONG person, just to satisfy that wish. If you say, "As long as he's breathing, I'll go out with him" then do not be surprised when the scum of the earth hits on you, or even worse, when you date or marry them! They have satisfied the goal you set for yourself.

Be realistic and practical, but do not sell yourself short. If your goal is to be married to Brad Pitt, that's great. Realize that in order to meet Brad, you have to get rid of his wife, you have to travel in his circles, you have to get past his security and most importantly: you have to be his type. Now if you want to take that down a notch and say, I want to marry a man who makes me feel the way I do about Brad Pitt, you are FAR more likely to find it. Remember that you may have to tailor yourself to fit the needs and wants of a man you find attractive. This does not mean selling yourself short, but accepting who you are now, and making

16

improvements along your journey. This does not mean having tons of plastic surgery. If you are a full figured lady, then dress the part, dress with style and flare. A French woman can walk down the street in the same suit and scarf as an American or British woman, but men will notice the French woman first. Men may even feel they are not worthy to approach her; because she will have the confidence to take a scarf and do something dramatic with it that will enhance her look. I'm not trying to speak down about American women exactly, but... Taking pride in your appearance is the outward sign that you are a strong, confident person with goals, dreams and a plan of how to achieve them.

I am speaking to those who feel it is perfectly acceptable to enter the grocery or pharmacy in stretch pants and a t-shirt covered with dog hair. STOP IT! You never know whom you will encounter, or where the man of your dreams may appear. Some women think, "If he likes me, it won't matter what I'm wearing." You are wrong. If what you are wearing is distracting from whom you want to be, he won't even notice you.

Most important of all, you have to love yourself. Let me say that again: YOU MUST LOVE YOURSELF FIRST. If you cannot look in the mirror and say that you are worthy and lovable, and BELIEVE IT, then no one else will believe it either. Sometimes you have to start from the outside, to repair the inside. Loving yourself is similar to a sales job, in that a salesperson is 100 times more likely to do well at selling, if they believe in the product. If you have ever watched late-night infomercials, there is one where a man sells a rotisserie oven. Within minutes of watching the "host" you are ready to pick up the phone and order half a dozen of the stupid oven things. I'm sure it is a great product, but the most important lesson to learn from the host, is not how to cook a chicken in less time and with less effort. The lesson to learn is that he BELIEVES this a revolutionary product that will make life easier for everyone who buys it. I actually think he is the inventor of the oven thing. But if he's not, he makes you feel like he is. This is the same enthusiasm that you must develop about yourself. YES, you must be enthusiastic about yourself – without being obnoxious.

There will be more about wardrobe, hair and makeup later, but just keep in mind you need to always be presentable (even after you get the ring on your finger).

My father taught me a meditation technique and I am modifying it here for our purpose:

> Close your eyes and picture simple darkness. Put everything else out of your mind. Any thoughts that come into your head, pictures or otherwise, put them out of your mind and focus on the soothing darkness of having closed eyes. Once you have achieved calm, imagine you are in a crowded event. You see the back of the head of the man who is coming into your life. He is seated, so you cannot see his height. You are a little ways away, so you cannot hear his voice clearly, but you are close enough to feel his presence.

What do you think he likes to do for fun? Is he polite to others at the party? Does he drink? Does he smoke? What type of clothes is he wearing to the event? What religion is he?

Now make notes on what you have seen and felt. This is the type of person who draws you to them. This is how you will begin to understand what attracts you to a person. He may have traits from previous men you have dated, a previous colleague from work, a professor from college, even another woman you know. The traits you like in a broad range of people will come together in the man you want to draw into your life. Try to avoid placing any restrictions on where you get these traits. There may be traits from your parents that you admire and hope to find in a potential mate. Do this meditation several times over several days, making notes after each one.

For the next meditation:

Close your eyes again and picture simple darkness. Put all other thoughts out of your mind. Any thoughts that come into your head, pictures or otherwise, put them aside and focus on the soothing darkness of having closed eyes. Once you have achieved calm, I want you to picture yourself at the mirror in the morning. Your new man is in the other room and you are looking great! Being together with another person, being a couple, really agrees with you. Even your friends comment on the way you seem so much happier.

Look into the mirror now. What are you wearing? How is your hair done, and has your weight changed since meeting the one? Has your body become more toned, because the two of you are out actually doing things together? What do you enjoy doing together? What scent do you wear when you are going out with him? Remember many men prefer fragrances that relate to food or nature, not heavy flowery scents. What is your favorite food and can you recall sharing it with your new man? If the favorite food involves chocolate, is it a dessert item you can smell and taste now, as you enjoy the feeling of being in love?

Think back over the weeks since you have met each other... Have you showered together? Have you played jokes on each other? What would you do if all of a sudden while you were in the shower a cup of cold water were dumped on your head? What would your new man do if you did that to him? Would you each laugh and plot your next prank or would you sulk and get angry?

Now look again in the mirror. Can you see why he loves you? Do you see the simple things about you - even with all your emotional/psychological baggage; can you see what makes you lovable? Can you see what your friends see: You + happy?

This exercise is critical. You must see your own happiness in your own mind for it to start being real to you. To attract people who bring joy, you most have joy to share.

Do these meditations over again, several times. Your internal feelings about yourself and the person you want to attract will take time to come out. This is not the way you have approached your search before, so this will take several sessions of meditation and reflection before you have a more complete image both of whom you are, and of the man will compliment your life.

Chapter 3
Defining Your Goal

Do you *REALLY* want to the tattoo covered biker guy? Are you *SURE* you want to date the pool guy? Would you *ACTUALLY* be happy with that rich geek with the bad hair and weird clothes?

You cannot achieve your goal until you have defined what exactly you want. The meditations from the last chapter will be a guide. But how can you expect to get something great, how will you recognize it, unless you know what you want?

One important aspect is that you need to recognize the patterns of your dating past. As I said in the last chapter, you have to look at your life and the attributes, which in another person will blend best with your life. Are you always attracted to the bad-boy? Do you always go after the model type and then get tossed aside later on? Do you look for wealth first and then realize that you are only another accessory for the guy? Recognizing your pattern is the first step in defining your goal-person. How do your self-perception and the perception of others impact how you define your goal?

For your next exercise, create a list of men you have dated. Then make notes next to each to identify traits about them; both good and bad. Be honest about what you recall and see if there are certain patterns or even one item that repeats. Ask your friends what they have seen. Give them a name of an ex of yours and ask them to come up with one or two words that fit him. They may recall more about your dating patterns because they see it all from a distance. They hear what you mention about the people you date, each time you are dating. Sometimes there is a clear pattern of attraction. This may be connected to the problems that develop in the relationship as it matures. You cannot marry the one who is a bad-boy all the time... Or you will be bailing him out of jail, and will have to raise the kids on your own. You may want a hint of bad-boy, or hell raiser. But you also want some saintliness mixed in there too.

Jeremy	Handsome, good cook, possessive, jealous
Bill	Tall, rich, overweight, talked with his mouth full
Mike	Outgoing, giving, caring, athletic, nag
Ronald	Rich, motivated, shallow, can't commit

Of course these are just examples to get you started. You will need to be far more detailed to discover the patterns.

Next we need to perform a goal exercise. What do you want? This is not a rhetorical question. I want you to write down, in great detail, exactly the type of person that you want. Beyond that, I want you to write down, in detail, where you see yourself going in the relationship with the person of your dreams.

For this exercise I want you to think about all the little things that you like in others that would be good qualities in a mate. Does height matter to you (If you are having children together, do you want them to be taller or shorter than you)? Do you like a strong personality that challenges you, or do you want to agree on so many levels that you feel a personality-mesh? Do you like the other person to be the strong personality?   Remember there is no judgment attached to this – it is about what you enjoy and feels right for you.

What does your new man smell like, when dressed for a night out with you? Is your new man husky or lean? Does that turn you on? Are they a different race than you? Are they much older or much younger?

List all the qualities you want in this ideal mate. Remember there are no preset boundaries, but also be realistic. If you write that he is a star NFL player, think at the same time where you encounter NFL players in your life. If you cross paths with famous athletes regularly, more power to you, and we can work from there. If your ideal mate is a famous model, then great for you. But think of how often you encounter famous models, how many there are and what they do for fun. Aim high with your first draft. Then go back and edit. I want you to realize that you deserve someone who is really great. You deserve a great man who will be everything you need. You will find the man who will challenge you when you need to be challenged. You will find the man who knows what you are about to say (and can kick you under the table, when it should not be said).

Be detailed about everything but the face. When you picture the person, I want you to imagine them facing away from you. This is important. You should not have a preconceived notion regarding the details of the face. Creating a face image keeps you from being open when people come into your life that may fit the profile you have created.   You don't want to eliminate a person, or discount them because you have envisioned George Clooney, Mark Consuelos, Blair Underwood, or Matthew McConaughey and then you never see anyone in the course of your life that fits that bill. Be detailed, but let the person turn out to be someone you would actually encounter in the course of your life.

Here is an example:

My new husband is average height range and professional. He speaks several languages and he loves me even more than I love him... He is so cuddly, affectionate and passionate. He just loves sex and is so willing to explore new things in and out of the bedroom. He is muscular, has a great build for his height, even stands out in a suit. People notice when he walks down the street or into a restaurant.

He is well educated with varied life experiences since college, including a diverse, eclectic, even fun background; like me but different. It is amazing that he has free time to spend with me, with such a great career. He is close to my age, same religion, and even spiritual. He is politically savvy and my whole family loves being around him just as he enjoys being with us. We have almost no arguments and I laugh way more then I ever have in my life before meeting him.

Even though I would probably have loved him if he had been broke, he is comfortably wealthy and very generous. He knows life without funds, but learned how to make a great living.

He loves family and fits in well with mine. He loves my dogs. Normally a guy like him would have an attitude, but he is not a jerk, to me or to anyone.

We each take time alone without it bothering either of us. This contributes to our time together.

He is an outdoorsman and loves travel even more than me. He has greatly encouraged me and even enabled, when he could, the amazing financial success I have had since meeting him.

We own a beautiful home. His excellent taste in music, wine, clothing, and even home décor sometimes conflicts with my quirkiness, but we are always able to work things out.

Gladly my new husband does not take any drugs.

I am so grateful now to have a person in my life that encourages me and helps me with the follow-through on my great ideas. His encouragement and perseverance continues to bring about lots of success, happiness and wealth, enabling me to live a life I never expected and share it with others I love. We now give away more each year than my entire income was in all the years before I met him.

This is the kind of detail you have to put into your plan.

Put everything in PAST TENSE. The reason for this is simple. In various research I have read, all the scientific evidence seems to come to the same conclusion: we only use 10% of our brains for conscious work. That means that the other 90% of the brain's power is the subconscious mind. Your subconscious mind does not know the difference between reality and fantasy, and will work for you either way you drive it[ii].

Think for a moment about how your body reacts while you are watching a scary movie. Your heart rate increases, your palms may sweat and you grab the armrests. At the scariest part, when something surprises you, you scream. Your conscious mind knows that what you are hearing is recorded sound. What your eyes are watching is simply flickering light, projected on a screen. But you have suspended your disbelief. You let your subconscious mind react as though the knife were actually coming down on a real live person in front of you. What we are doing within the exercise above is harnessing that amazing power that is NINE TIMES more powerful than your thinking, everyday mind. You are forcing your subconscious to accept that you already have the ideal mate in your life, and then force your habits to adapt to the new reality. The more you read your goal over and over, the more it will be believable to you and the more real it becomes to your subconscious mind.

This is applicable to any goals you want to achieve, so take the concept and create your new reality.

Remove your limitations by retraining yourself and training your subconscious mind to work on creating a new reality.

In Steve Sacks book, *The Mate Map*, he outlines various criteria and the way of prioritizing what you find is most important in a mate. It is a great book. Steve has his readers list the qualities they like in a person and then has exercises to help decide what is the absolute priority in a mate. Next he has the reader list what qualities are more flexible.

As I have said, in my own experience advising friends and listening, and in research for this book – the qualities you like may go out the window when you meet someone who makes you say "WOW". The person you meet may not have the weight, height or eye color you envisioned in the perfect mate, but they make you laugh so hard your face hurts. They may hold your hand and you feel the love you have not known with any other. Then you just know this is the person for you.

As you move through life, people touch your soul in many ways: a teacher who takes a little extra time with you, a parent who is your favorite (even though you never told them), a co-worker who helped you with a project expecting nothing in return, a stranger who stopped to help you change a tire on your car on a hot summer day, a person who defended you in a conversation that you overheard without them knowing. The qualities these people had that touched your soul are the same traits that you may not list or articulate, but matter when choosing a mate. It is these little things: concern, caring, tenderness, protectiveness, that are not things you can see when

you meet a person, but you discover along the way –
these qualities are what matter in the long haul.

Write down your dream description and recite it
every day.

Chapter 4
Preparing/Presenting Yourself

The charms of the divine woman must have been irresistible, if even 'the wisest men' were ready to do anything in their desire to abandon themselves, even for a few moments, to their trained embraces"
G.R. Tabouts, The Private Life of Tutankh amon.

I love that quote. You should be irresistible!

Never leave the house looking a mess. And to those that say the perfect guy will love me no matter how I look, I say sure, but only AFTER he has come to know and love you. First impressions are everything.

We have covered a lot of things so far. But, what matters most when you first meet are in fact, first impressions. Almost everyone evaluates your appearance from the outside in. This is because the most important part of a first impression is how you look. I recently attended a lecture by Olivia Fox Cobane (The Charisma Coach). She teaches networking for corporations and business people. Ms. Fox Cobane quotes from a study by the Massachusetts Institute of Technology, which states that a first impression is made in TWO SECONDS!!! Further research indicates that this first impression can last as long as six months. Whether you are a creationist or an evolutionist - we humans are developed and perfectly adapted to Stone-Age life. That's right, STONE AGE. The millions of cells and synapses of your brain are firing a million times a second and are set to the Stone Age, when you had to react in two seconds or die[iii]. Your mind determines first – SIZE, (can I beat them up or should I run), second, your mind determines race. This is a fact, whether you like it or not, and the reason is quite simple: In Stone Age times you had determine in two seconds whether the person standing in front of you is of your tribe, or not your tribe. Your reaction to the person in front of you is based on these immediate observations. Of course what you want to do in order to blend in with a different tribe is common sense – **wardrobe**! If you want to meet a certain type of person – you have to learn to blend in with the modern version of their tribe! If you want a man who is all about golf – you have to learn to dress the part, then talk the talk. Learn the language of a golfer ("Hole in one" is a big moniker). If you are a woman seeking to marry a computer geek in Silicon Valley, blend with the geeks in their t-shirts, Toyota Prius and loose (not baggy) jeans or khakis. Read trade journals or magazines so you can pick up the language of the computer geeks.

If you want to meet a lawyer or a doctor, you have to learn where they go in their off time, as well as how they dress for work and play. Go to lunch where the lawyers lunch, dressed as they dress, then make sure to show up at the Bar Association's Holiday Benefit or some other similar function.

Ok, here is the part where a makeover is necessary so you are able to attract "the one". Now don't get all bent out of shape because I say you need a makeover - I don't know you. But EVERYONE could stand for some improvement. If you feel that there is nothing to improve upon, think again!

You need to have someone completely objective who can look at you, hear you speak, see you walk and watch you dine and interact with strangers. If you are abusive to the help, you will most likely be abusive in a relationship. Perhaps the abuse will not be physical, but it may be verbal or mental. If you ignore or dismiss the staff in a restaurant, you will probably do that with anyone who is not in a position to further your wants and needs.

As for hair, makeup and clothing – I want you to call a few Personal Coaches or look up First Impression Management or a similar company that will evaluate you. If you walk into a department store and ask for a makeover, you may be bombarded with products from that store, whether they will improve your look or not. If you cannot afford a personal coach or stylist, department stores can be a great help. If you use department store personal shoppers, take the advice with a bit of skepticism, and get a second opinion!

A reputable personal coach will aid in the improvement of your appearance by looking at you as a product. This is not meant to be offensive. If you are walking around like an outdated box of cereal in the same package from 1965, how will anyone know that you are current, exciting and ready to be tasted? The personal coach will be objective and may very well offend you at first. Tell them upfront that you can handle the truth, and then be strong. If you are wearing clothing you made yourself or spandex pants and oversized sweatshirts (first you should be shot... just kidding), the personal coach should be able to tell you that your look simply will not work – HOWEVER, in exchange for dealing with the pain of truth, you can expect them to have answers! You can expect the personal coach to advise you on what you need to change or fine tune, in order to fix your look.

Here is a breakdown of the process:

Visual Transformation:

- Color Analysis
- Figure Analysis and Report - Few of us are proportioned perfectly, but we can achieve the illusion of balance.
- Hair Cut and Styling review
- Wardrobe Plan
- Makeup Makeover
- Dressing Guidelines
- The Psychological Effects of Color

- Color Analysis -

The coach should be able to hold fabric across in front you – perhaps in a mirror so you can see. The various colors of fabric will let you see what works and what does not. You may even have this recorded on video. Video is notoriously unforgiving and will even add 10lbs that you don't want! Videotape yourself with various colors surrounding your face and you will see what is complimentary and what should be avoided.

- Figure Analysis –

The next part should be a figure analysis. I know that the men are not so worried – but they should be. Since the 1980's women have become much more interested in a guy who is physically healthy looking. The United States has enough over-fat people. Don't be one of them, if you can avoid it. I am not saying overweight because I don't really think that term applies. People with big bones or large figures can still be healthy looking, attractive and dress well. One of my dearest friends in high school and college was a very large woman. I never really noticed. She was gorgeous, dressed well and was absolutely one of the funniest, most charming people on the planet. She always appeared healthy and happy. What I later learned was that she was having health issues related to her size. After she had lost over 150lbs I learned that she was having knee problems from her previous weight. I weighed 140lbs around that time, just so you know. My point here is that you should look and feel healthy, if you want others to have that impression of you. I always had that impression of my friend, and so did the various men who were always after her. If you want to get in better shape and help create a positive self-image – I highly recommend it. I personally work out about 4-5 days a week, for forty-five minutes to an hour. Working out is a great stress release and a break in the day to take care of myself. Exercise also boosts your energy, and your self-confidence. It is hard to be depressed when your heart rate is elevated form working out.

- Hair Cut and Styling - (This is a big one)
Both men and women need to have a hairstyle that is both flattering to their face and build, but also current. Speak to a hairdresser before they cut or reshape your hair. Find out what they feel will be most flattering to you, and try to visualize it first. You may even go so far as to try a wig and see if the new style suits you before you commit.

- Wardrobe Plan -

Here is where a Personal Coach or Personal Shopper steps in and helps. You may have great taste in some things or you may not. But a qualified Personal Coach or Personal Shopper with references is worth their weight in gold. Since they are not making money off the wardrobe purchases, they are able to be objective and guide you in the direction you intend to go. Remember that wardrobe is your key to fitting into the "tribe" you seek to join. If your ideal partner is a lawyer, you will need to have a few items of clothing that a lawyer wears, so that you can fit in at business functions and the like.

- Makeup -

Again, here you will need an expert. You may rely on a friend, if they are in the makeup business or a professional makeup artist. In most cases you can experiment with different styles by speaking to a makeup counter person at a department store or Sephora store. Let them show you their products and what they can do to create the look you need. By prepared to either tip or purchase products, sometimes both. Bring a friend who can also be objective.

- Dressing Guidelines -

As I have said, the goal now is dressing to fit into the lifestyle of the type of person you want to meet and the person you want to be. You may want to look at trade journals or magazines related to the field of your target partner or your own goal lifestyle. See how the people in the advertisements are dressed. There are many ways to look like you stepped out of a magazine, but by putting together less expensive options.

- Psychological Effects of Color -

As your decide what you will use as your signature color, be aware of the meaning of colors. In some cultures, red means "Stop" – however in the same cultures, red means Love. In China, red is good luck! Here are some examples:

Blue: Sky, Sea, Water, Religious feeling, Peace, Faith, Stability, Melancholy, Trust, Loyalty, Wisdom, Tranquility, Integrity
Red: Fire, Love, Passion, Energy, Revolution, Anger, Power, Debt, Danger, Heat, Warning
Yellow: Energy, Sun, Happiness, Cheery, Creativity
Purple: Royalty, Power, Nobility, Spirituality, Luxury
Green: Money, Growth, Environmentally friendly, Fertility, Envy, Spring, Freshness, Stability, Loyal, Healing
Orange: Joy, Sunshine, Creativity, Determination, Success, Encouragement, Energy, Autumn, Construction
Brown: Conservative, Stable, Outdoors, Fall, Earth, Organic

Keep these color connections in mind as you pick your wardrobe and even when you paint the interior of your home. Colors will affect not just others, but will affect your own mood and happiness.

Making the outside "you" ready for a special new man in your life will also help with the inside. When we feel attractive, we are more likely to be happy and confident with others. This in turn draws others to you.

Chapter 5
Dining Etiquette

OMG, Please use a napkin!

Relationships are developed and strengthened in social situations. Mastering the art of fine dining will make you appear worldly and sophisticated. Remember, whether you are the host or the guest, you have a responsibility to ensure the overall success of any event.

Some things you need to understand are the duties and responsibilities of the guest and host:

- Sitting down at the table
- Posture
- American versus Continental eating style
- Proper use of flatware
- Using your napkin
- Excusing yourself
- Dinner table talk
- Talking to servers
- Reaching for items
- Asking for what you need
- Removing food from your mouth when food is too hot
- Catsup and other sauces
- Using bread to clean the plate
- Drinking too much
- Dropped flatware or food
- Food spilled on the table
- Used flatware - what to do with it
- Sharing food
- Smoking at the table

If you are the hostess entertaining – even though you are trying to impress the man of your dreams – you must remember that your primary duty is to make sure your guest or guests are happy.

Your duties in seating are generally to place people in such a way as to create conversation. Placing the supermodel next to the world leader is always a good idea, unless they are from opposing parties. Also keep in mind that you have to then place the world leader's wife near a hot tennis pro or a hunky wrestler. Now also bear in mind that the most important guest is always placed at your right hand.

Posture – is something that I really don't want to go into, but it has to be mentioned. A slouching posture is a sign (whether correct or not). Poor posture is perceived as a sign of unhappiness/lack of confidence. There are many other connotations, but for our purpose of preparing you for dating – unhappiness is clearly the more important. You want to exude happiness. You want to stand tall, stand firm and sit upright, ready for anything.

If you want to appear more worldly, check your eating style. American versus Continental eating style – Many of you may not notice the difference in your guests. I was actually approached a few years ago by the waitress in a restaurant in downtown Nashville. I eat in the Continental manner, simply because it makes more sense with food that involves cutting. With Continental style, one holds the fork in the left hand and the knife in the right. One holds the food steady with the fork in the left and cuts with the right. American style would have you then switch the fork to the right hand before eating. This is a waste of time. Just take the bite of food off the fork with the tines aimed down, and go back to cutting more food - Just my thoughts. Regarding catering or serving of food at a more formal event, remember there are several forms:

Russian Service: Trays of food are brought to each place at the table and guests serve themselves from the trays.

French Service: Trays of food are brought to each place and the server places the food on each plate.

"Table d'Hôte": In the US, this is called Family-style, where dishes are placed on the table and passed around for diners to serve themselves.

Flatware is sometimes a daunting thing for people used to just one fork, one knife and no spoon. Don't be put off. There is a simple rule that governs flatware. The farther out the flatware is from the plate, the earlier in the meal it is to be used. If we start with an appetizer and then a soup, the farthest flatware from the plate should be a salad fork (slightly smaller) and a soup spoon (slightly larger). Then we move on to a fish course and you will find a fish fork and perhaps a fish knife. The fish knife is flat and larger then a regular knife. The fish fork has side tines that are thicker. I'm sure you know what a steak knife looks like, so I won't go into that. Dessert forks and spoons are often placed at the top of the plate. If there is a staff, these are moved down to the sides when the last dinner plate or charger (that big plate under the regular plate) is removed.

Dining napkins are an essential part of the dining experience. Even if you are sharing a club sandwich, sitting on a picnic table by a lake, napkins are important. Paper napkins have their uses, but cloth napkins are preferable. Do not wipe your mouth on your sleeve or anything else. This is the point of the napkin. If something tastes terrible and you can't suffer through it, spit the offending item into your napkin discretely. If you have to sneeze, you may use your napkin, but do not place it on the table afterward. You do not want to share your germs with everyone.

Always excuse yourself if you have to leave the table while dining with others. This applies, even if everyone has completed his or her meal. At large gatherings, it is only necessary to excuse yourself with the people at your table, or the people on either side of your seat. You do not need to tell anyone where you are going. We who are still eating or talking really don't care. Your date does not need to know that you have to use the rest room. They will figure it out, just say "excuse me."

As for conversation, polite people avoid discussing anything vulgar during a meal. This may include bodily functions, surgery or anything including blood or human or animal waste. Some people suggest avoiding politics as well, but that is more of a situational recommendation. Stay with topics like travel, world news, local news, or anecdotal stories from your past or that of your dinner companion.

Always be polite to the servers in a restaurant or in someone's home. Even when you have bad service, there are diplomatic ways of handling it. How you treat the staff, is indicative of how you treat others. Your dinner companion or your friends will notice how you treat the staff. If the service is particularly bad, mention it to the manager as you are leaving. In the US, tipping is virtually mandatory. But you may tip lightly when the service is very bad. Tip generously when the service is good, and be sure to mention your great service to a manager or host as you leave.

I know I am running on and on here about manners – but they do make a difference. Having good manners and educating your children to have them makes the world a better place.

Reaching for items at the table can be tricky in some situations. If you have to fully extend your arm to reach something, you may be better off asking someone who is closer to pass the item. It is better to have something passed, then to knock over a drink and ruin the meal. Generally it is better to pass something and set it down on the table, close to the person who requested it. That way the chances of dropping the item during the pass are diminished.

Ask politely for what you need, whether it is asking for more to drink or requesting for a dining neighbor to pass the salt.

Removing items from your mouth is a delicate procedure best handled behind the curtain of a napkin and should be placed in it. In China, it is not acceptable to touch anything that has been inside your mouth. In the Chinese culture, this dining etiquette requires one to spit out bones, etc. Here in the US, we may spit out items, but we try to spit them into a napkin. I don't want to see what was just in your mouth, thanks!

If food is too hot, blowing on the food bothers some people. Personally, I think it is better to blow on the food than to burn your tongue. The alternative is to just talk for a few minutes and let the food cool down.

Catsup and other sauces are often available and may be used. If you are a person who requires catsup on food in order to eat it, try to get rid of that habit. Putting catsup on most things offends the cook, unless it is a hot dog or hamburger.

I am trying not the ramble here, but to give you a quick rundown of dining etiquette to avoid embarrassment. If you learned all this already, you can move on. For the rest, read on:

Never use your bread to clean your plate. You may dip bread into a sauce or broth, but do not mop your plate with the bread.

Drinking alcohol is another delicate matter when dining out with new people. Some folks are offended by drinking, while others feel you are offending them if you refrain. This is best handled on a case-by-case basis. However, it is best to avoid getting drunk with new people or on a date. First, you probably will have to drive, and second you may say things you will regret later. If you start to feel that a drink is kicking in, switch to drinking water or a cola for a while. Pace your drinking so you do not get drunk.

If you drop food or a utensil during a meal there are several rules for managing the situation. In a restaurant, leave the item – they have staff to pick it up later. In a person's home, look to your host/hostess first to see what they expect. Generally speaking, you do not want to place something back on the table once it has been on the floor. Leave it, or pick it up and go rinse it off.

If you drop food on the table, you may place it back on your plate, but leave it near the edge.

Once you have completed your dinner, place the utensils on the diagonal across the plate. If the plate were a clock, the top of the utensils should be at 10 or 11:00, with the base at 4 or 5:00. This is a Western culture indication that you have finished eating. Unless you worked as a waiter or caterer, you may not have learned this. But this practice allows a server to pick up your plate with one hand, placing a thumb on the utensils to keep from dropping them.

As for sharing food – this again is entirely situational. I would not suggest sharing food at a large event with anyone unless they are family or your date. Never expect a person to eat from your fork. If you want to share a taste of your delicious meal, cut a small portion off and place it on the edge of your friend's plate. They can then taste it when they have a chance. Desserts are often shared, but avoid using another person's fork, unless you are feeding your own children. Men (other than your own father or brothers) who eat from your fork will expect sex, just so you know.

Smoking at the table was once part of every meal all over the world. But in recent years smoking has passed to something that is done after a meal, outside where the smoke will not bother others. I suggest you avoid smoking at the table as it distracts from the tasting of food for most people. I am not a smoker.

Dining out with others, in a group or one-on-one is supposed to be a pleasurable experience. Sharing a meal is a chance to get to know another person and learn more about them. Follow these simple guidelines and others will be relaxed and able to open up to you.

Chapter 6
Your Home Environment

As my dad often yelled, "Clean your room!" Many parents lecture they children to make the bed and clean their room. From a practical sense, they were right. Now that you are an adult, you should not need anyone to tell you this, you should know to do it anyway.

Your home is a reflection of who you are on the inside. If your home is a disaster area, then your life is probably one as well. If you can't seem to keep the dishes from piling up in the sink, then your life is probably piling up around you just the same. This applies to both men and women. How you keep your home is a sign to others of how you care about yourself. This may not be true for you, but it is true when it comes to the impressions people get when they see your home the first time.

Certainly you have walked into homes and smelled wonderful candles and used the plush towels in the bathroom and thought, wow, these people live well. Do the same. You don't have to go into debt, but keep your home clean and neat – even smelling nice, and you will feel infinitely better about yourself.

One of my friends was talking online for quite some time with a person. Both parties had busy schedules and so online dating websites seemed to be the only thing they could both fit in. So after some exchanges, my friend traveled out from Manhattan to Queens to meet the person. They agreed to meet in the guy's apartment and go from there. The building appeared a bit shabby as my friend arrived and was buzzed into the lobby. That can be okay. There are some incredible apartments in shabby old buildings in New York. Then the door to the apartment opened, and all was lost. The guy stood there in a dirty t-shirt and boxer shorts. It got worse. My friend (not yet in full panic mode) stepped into the apartment. Inside there was a sofa turned up on one end, the fabric covering, had been shredded by cat claws. On the floor rested a soiled mattress with only a top sheet crumpled on one end. Strewn across the floor were old burger wrappers, French fry cartons, bits of paper, dirty clothes, etc. We can laugh about this now, but at the time, my friend was in full horror at the filth when she heard the words: "Can you take your shoes off." Immediately the thought went through her head, "If I take my shoes off, my feet will get dirty."

She turned to the guy and said: "I don't think this is gonna work." Then she turned and left.

Clearly this is an extreme example, but you need to be prepared for a visit.

Even if you did not grow up in a perfectly clean home like "Leave it to Beaver" or "The Cosby Show" – your can create your own neat and clean environment. One of the best things to do to get an idea of what your place looks like in an objective manner is to photograph or videotape your rooms. When you are not standing in the room, you can see how cluttered rooms become. If you have ever seen the show "Sell This House", then you know that clutter in the home and dark rooms turns people off. In the show, they are trying to attract buyers to a home. But in your case you want to attract both friends and a partner in life. This applies to women as well as men. If you can't be objective, show the video or photos to a friend or a decorator at a home improvement store. Tell them you want suggestions on creating clean lines like a showroom for selling your place. You do not need to tell them that you are not actually looking to sell the house. You are looking to sell a potential companion on the idea of having you as their mate.

Tons of small objects, photos, stacks of books or other things – all contribute to a messy look and will turn people away. Put things away, throw things out and keep surfaces like tables, counters, dressers all clear of clutter. If there are things you use every day, then create space in a drawer or hide them in an attractive box. This is great for remote controls, wallets, keys, watches, etc. Use solid colors for drapes, sheets and big furniture like sofas. This will create more of a clean line. Excessive amounts of pillows on the bed or on the sofa are clutter when you glance at a room quickly. I know they look great to you and the designers who placed them in the department store display. But resist the temptation to have so many pillows that no one can sit down on the sofa or the bed.

Never leave the house without making your bed if you can avoid it. This is doubly true when you are actually dating someone. If they are lucky enough for you to invite them over, you want to give the impression that you always take pride in yourself and your home.

As for your kitchen, you should have something to eat: eggs, juice, sausage and you should at least know how to prepare a full breakfast. Again, I am not saying this just because you are female. It is always a good thing to be able to make breakfast for someone you love and serve it to them in bed; or allow them to make breakfast in bed for you. This also means you must have the cookware, and eating utensils to cook and serve it, so that a wonderful meal can be enjoyed. That means a complete set, no mismatched or chipped plates. That means no mismatched eating utensils. Your glassware should not be a collection of old jars. Since household items have become very inexpensive in various mega stores, you have no excuse. There is no excuse to not have some drink options as well; canned drinks can keep for years.

Next is the bathroom. If your mother would be horrified at your bathroom's lack of tidiness, then so will your date. If you have a lot of products on the counter, buy a cabinet to hide them. If your medicine cabinet is too small, buy one of the large, three panel type (I use one). Preferably the only thing that should be on your counter is soap. I prefer liquid soap in a pump so there is no mess. Your towels should be neat and the floor MUST BE CLEAN.

Make sure there is not hair everywhere and only hang up your delicates to dry overnight, or while you are at home. Guys do not want to walk in to use the restroom and be looking at your undergarments (well some men do). If you have a man around, make sure to clean the entire floor and also clean the walls or cabinet sides around the toilet. There is always splatter when urinating from a standing position and you may not even notice it. It will smell. To both men and women – the practice of leaving the toilet seat up "For a lady" is ridiculous. Close the toilet, close the cabinets, and close your drawers. No one wants to look down into your toilet – even though I expect it to be sparkling clean. It has a lid, close it. This is especially true in a small bathroom where objects tend to drop, bounce once off the counter and land "PLOP" into the open toilet. Enough said.

If you have pets, bathe them regularly and vacuum constantly. No one wants to walk into a home that smells of dog, cat, litter box, birdcage, etc. Even fish tanks can attain a smell if not cleaned. People will be put off if they go to sit in your home and become covered in dog or cat hair, or can't handle the smell.

When you are dating, and even after you find a special person to share your life, you must make the extra effort to create an environment in your home where other people feel comfortable and welcome. If you have piles of CDs on the floor or stacks of newspapers and clutter – buy cabinets or storage bins. Find a way to keep your clutter to a minimum.

Take pride in your home. It is an extension of taking pride in you. I know one married man who puts scented oil warmers all over his home, even in the garage. He says he likes the smell and that his wife is just as likely to spend time together with him in the garage, as he is spending time with her in the kitchen when she is cooking. PS. He does the dishes when she cooks.

Chapter 7
Plan Out a Process

As I said, you need to have a clear understanding of what you want in a mate. If you are interested in someone who is into horses, than keep in mind you have to put yourself in a horse-friendly environment. I have met people in Los Angeles that love horses, but never took the time to go riding in Griffith Park. Many people don't realize that Griffith Park in LA was donated specifically for horse riding along scenic trails; thus there is a riding camp for the curious and the horse enthusiast. In New York, you can ride in Forest Hills Park, Van Cortlandt Park and even in Prospect Park in Brooklyn. If horses are an interest, make it a part of your life. You will meet many new people along the way.

This holds true with most other interests. If you were on the tennis team in high school, but have become one of those people who come home, eat and sit in front of the television – STOP IT NOW. Get up and get out, you are not going to meet anyone new by sitting in your living room.

What you need to do is create a cohesive plan to carry out the search and seizure of your future mate. Now I know that may sound extreme. But if you truly want to attract, meet and capture the one, then this is the mentality you must have. Now, I want you to take the written description of your ideal mate, and add to that list, places where you think that type of person spends his time. If your ideal man is a fireman, start going to fire department picnics and fundraisers for the Fireman's Fund, or the like. If you are not a church regular, but your ideal mate is a person with a strong religious or moral background, join a church, mosque, temple or synagogue. You may not need to attend all the services, but certainly you want to stop by the socials, picnics or holiday celebrations.

Deciding where to go is a big part of the process. Often, meeting people by volunteering brings you into a different world than your normal day might. If you can spare the time, volunteer for a museum, botanical garden, hospital, or other worthy cause. You are opening yourself up to a new area to meet both a potential mate and also new friends. Generally, larger charities also have dances and events that will help you in your quest.

Another way to meet your potential mate is going to a specific type of health club or gym. This activity will place you around people who are active and are concerned with good health. If you want to meet a person of modest income level, then you will go to fitness clubs like 24hr Fitness or Bally's. If a higher income level is your goal, you will join a club like Equinox or Lifetime Fitness. This may be out of reach for some financially, but unlike one-on-one training, you have a chance to meet others in the group environment of a health club.

I also recommend cruises (I recommend this for single men all the time). There are usually more women of a certain income level traveling alone on a cruise, who want to be pampered and spoiled. Because it is a safe environment, they are relaxed and open to meeting new people. This is particularly true for women over 30 who make a certain level of income and want to take a trip where they feel safe and secure. There are so many women traveling alone on cruises that cruise lines have hired single men to dance and dine with the women on board. This keeps them coming back. I know of one older gentleman who tours all over the world at the expense of the cruise lines. He is gay, so there is no mistake that he is not on board to do anything other than dance, dine and flirt with the older ladies aboard. For a single man, cruises are a great place to meet a special lady, and I recommend that men go alone or with their children. Take a cooking class or join an archeology lecture, as you cruise toward an ancient Mayan ruin. If you are lucky, you will have a companion to go with you by the time you reach your destination. Certain cruise lines cater to a particular audience. Some travelers will be seen in black tie at dinner on one of Cunard Lines ships like the Queen Mary II or the Queen Victoria. Those with children are more likely to travel on Disney or Celebrity Cruise lines.

Golf is a very particular outing that brings together a lot of singles. Many are very passionate about their game and playing golf is very stratified into levels of skill. Do not let this deter you. If you love golf, join a golf club and spend time at the club as well. If you are a single woman hoping to meet a man, joining a women's group is not the way to go. Women's groups are great for making friends and taking trips to play in tournaments, but it is not a place to meet the opposite gender.

Tennis follows the same rules as golf; it is a great way to meet people. If you can play tennis or want to learn, join a group and make friends. If you can find a tennis group that is mixed in terms of genders and has both singles and married people, then you are in an even better position to meet eligible singles with a common interest.

Take a class; this can be a night school at a university or community college. But it can also include many other venues. Community Centers all across the US offer classes in painting, sculpture, crafts, basket weaving, knitting, cooking, acting and more. The list is endless. If you are an outdoor enthusiast, take a rock-climbing course or join a rock-climbing club. Remember, if your budget is limited, you can often volunteer for groups, to pay your way. Community theater groups need lots of volunteers and if you are shy, there are plenty of behind-the-scenes roles. You can help build sets, bake goods for a fundraiser, distribute flyers, arrange lights, or whatever may be needed to get you involved.

Support the arts in other ways in your community to open your life to meeting new people. Volunteer with your local arts fair – set up tents or tables, staff the information booth, pass out flyers, post notices in your neighborhood and meet new people.

Get involved and get off your butt and out of your house to break up your comfort level. Your comfort zone often keeps you from connecting with new people.

Do not let this level of involvement or adventure scare you off. If you are intimidated by the idea of doing these things on your own, bring a friend along. The friend does not need to be single to join you. Activities like I have described above, will only contribute to a relationship. Your friends can come as a couple to participate, or one of them can join you. If only one comes, at least they will have a new experience to share with their partner, when they get home. They also will have something to talk about as they snuggle on the sofa late at night.

Chapter 8
Building a Network
Leading to The One

TALK to people! Introduce yourself, to women and to men and BE NICE! You never know who might be the connection of a lifetime.

Networking is important in both your business and personal life. You network and make friends by communicating. You can either use networking to lead to "the one" through introduction or by approaching people directly. Let me reiterate, whatever type of person you wish to meet: bankers, construction workers, athletes... go to places where they dine, dress as they dress, or dress to attract them. Make sure to show up at a holiday benefit, or some other similar function, which they attend. Sometimes you can be talking only a few moments with a new person and their friend(s) will interrupt, thus allowing you the opportunity to meet a whole new set of people. Through this introduction you may meet someone for dating, while not truly knowing the person that has introduced you. You may have only just met them and started talking – but others will perceive you as a friend of their friend, thus letting their guard down.

This is one of the best introductions you can have with a complete stranger. You have the opportunity to tell them as much or as little as you want. Since the person who actually introduced you only knows you superficially, you are beginning with a clean slate. Do not lie here – you have the opportunity to talk about your strong points and listen attentively as the other person does the same. Listening to others is very important, and men in particular are often only listening superficially. As a woman, remember this in a conversation. Keep the man engaged and notice if his mind wanders. Networking is about actually listening and providing a value to your new acquaintance. Even if the man in front of you is not your ideal mate, he may have a friend who is!

Networking is not just about the introduction it is the process of maintaining relationships over time. To network properly you need to provide value to others and thus making you, invaluable. If you meet an executive whom you notice shuns coffee at corporate meetings. You make note of it and when you have a chance, offer her tea instead. Send a gift box of assorted teas! I am not saying that you as a woman are placing yourself as the server, but you are making note of things that a person likes, and then fulfilling it. This makes you invaluable, memorable and people will come to you for answers, ideas and suggestions. If she knows you are single, she will also be much more likely to arrange for you to meet her eligible friends.

As Olivia Fox-Cobain says in her lectures on networking: When you notice a man has an interest in classic cars, you can "rip and send." This is the most flattering way to get a person to notice you were listening and paying attention to them. When you see an article about an upcoming classic car rally, you rip the article out and mail it to your new friend with a note. Tell him you weren't sure if he saw the article and you thought of him. When your favorite hairdresser loves cross-country cycling and there is an article about local trails, you rip and send to her.

Remember, she will think of you later, when an attractive single man comes in and happens to be your type.

If you hear that a person loves horses, you will make a mental note and remember to bring up horses the next time you have contact with them. If you receive a business card, feel free to make notes on the back of the card. If a person mentions they love traveling or architecture, feel free to rip-and-send something relating to their interest. By doing this, you have provided a value to your new acquaintance.

Pay attention in your networking or at various events, when you volunteer, or at your golf outing, or rock climbing. See who best matches, not just your physical desires, but find out who matches your ideals. Find out who makes you laugh, or if you are a person who likes to whine – find a compatriot with whom you can commiserate!

After you have eyed a few potentials, follow through by putting yourself out there, communicate and socialize. Use your network to find out if he is interested.

As we all know, if you are to be taken seriously as a potential mate, being introduced by someone who knows the person you want to meet is priceless. So do your homework, work the room, and pay attention. Who is a friend, or friend of a friend of the person in whom you are interested? Now, go to work. This is true for women, not just men. Men may avoid being introduced and feel that it may damage their macho image, allow him his ego. Have someone introduce you so that he is not "hitting on" you, it's just a casual introduction.

Networking at Events

So, how does one evaluate and strategically position themselves at an event to meet "the one"? What is the best location to meet a person of interest?

- Entrance?
- Seated at a table?
- Near the guest speaker?
- Buffet table?

You are at an evening event. You are mingling. How do you navigate the room in the most effective and efficient way possible, yet allowing yourself to meet potentials? First, there are two schools of thought: While working a room, some people say that having a drink in your hand is the proper way (always the left, so that your right hand is not damp or cold from the glass when you shake hands). Others say, keep your hands free so that there is nothing to interfere with talking, and nothing to spill when you have to squeeze past people.

I am of the former school: this also allows you an escape to refresh your glass, in the event the person you are talking to becomes boring, or you spot a person of interest from earlier in the evening. Now lets say you have zoned in on the person you want to meet. How do you meet them at this event? Where should you stand so that there is no doubt that you will meet? The buffet is the place to be, but even more specifically, stand near the dessert table. Desserts are also a perfect conversation starter.

After people have eaten, their endorphin levels are higher. Very few people hate desserts, so take your place and start chatting.

Where To Network

As for others with whom you should network: Hairdressers are notorious connectors. Keep them on your good side. Actually lots of people in the service industry are great connectors if you take the time to speak to them. Talk to your dry cleaner or even your pharmacist. They know who is single and who is married.

Talk to and network with:
- Friends/Relatives
- Former employers
- Former co-workers
- Classmates from school
- Members of your political party
- Members of your church
- Members of your social club(s)
- Present or former teachers
- Neighbors
- People in your athletic club
- People on your sports team
- Members of a professional group
- People who sell things: stores, insurance, etc.
- Fraternity/sorority members
- Teachers/advisors

These are all people who know a lot of people. They can be your eyes and ears helping you look for what you want. I do not mean that you run all over town telling everyone you are single and on the hunt. I am suggesting that you actually get to know the people around you. In conversation, you may mention that you are now open to dating. Then you can mention the type of man you like.

Even sitting on a plane can be a great place to network and meet people. Plenty of people sit in silence on a plane; most are lonely even though there are a hundred people surrounding them.

You can judge the level of interest in talking. If they are working on the plane, or listening to earphones, they are not open to discussion. If they are not otherwise occupied, say hello, introduce yourself; you never know who they are or whom they may know. This can be a business connection or a dating connection. I met a woman on Jury Duty once who later set me up on a date!!!

Chapter 9
Market Yourself Right

You don't need a billboard on a major highway to market yourself as a single person, ready to settle down.

Marketing is letting people know about your product. Marketing is NOT selling. So when you are marketing yourself, you are putting yourself out into the single world and letting others know that you are available for dating. If your intention is to get married and/or settle into a long-term relationship, then this must be clear in everything you do. There are many methods of marketing yourself, but if you are not clear on the actual product – nothing will work.

If you have in your head that a long-term relationship is what you seek, but you will sleep with everyone until then, you are sending mixed signals. If you want something permanent, then you cannot allow those who seek something temporary to distract you from your goal along the way. I am not saying don't go out and I'm not saying don't have sex. But what I am saying is that if you do this while your goal is a long-term relationship, then you diminish and dilute the achievement and direction. Here we are looking at you as a product to be marketed. So you cannot have a reputation for being easy. If you have a sexual encounter, be discrete. Your focus is creating the image that you are marrying material, not just one-night-stand material.

The Millionaire Matchmaker, Patti Stanger says that some people use sex as part of the getting-to-know-you process. I am not trying to judge here, but if you hold back from jumping in the sack, at least a few dates, you will see a completely different side of the person. You will find them more likely to consider you serious about wanting something long term.

Marketing yourself is a combination of presenting yourself in the correct manner, networking and using methods of advertising. These outward signs can be as simple as not wearing a ring on your finger, or not driving to an event with a friend of the opposite gender. You want people to know you are single and not think that this friend is actually your spouse.

When you are marketing a company you do the following things:
• Identify appropriate prospects.
• Effectively communicate corporate or product image and capabilities of your firm.
• Create/emphasize an appeal factor, a differentiation factor about your company or product.
• Perfect your customer service.
• Request feedback from clients on a regular basis.
• Anticipate and meet needs of clients.

So when marketing yourself, you need to think like a business. In terms of marketing, a company wants to focus on positioning – something that actually happens in the mind of the consumer. Does the buyer pick Tide® over Wisk® or Era®? This is brand positioning. Where does the product fall in order of priority in the mind of the consumer?

Keep these key marketing principals in mind as you decide what you will do to market yourself in the singles world:

1. Brand – who are you to others, how are you perceived on first impression, what do long-term friends think about you, what effect are you having on others (positive or negative), what is your value?

2. Positioning - something that takes place in the mind of the customer in a business situation– talk to a matchmaker, put out a profile online, join singles groups, go to bars, join a club. More importantly, do things you enjoy that involve getting out of the house or the office, unless your home and office have a ready supply of new single people.

3. Think about how singles pick the one with whom the will go out (in business this would be figuring out why and how customers buy one brand of product over the other) – get to know the criteria and processes your target single person goes through. What are the factors that influence their choices? Proximity, height/weight, hair color?

4. Competitors - who they are (not always obvious), their likely actions, what should you do or not do to be the first choice, ahead of the other singles out there?

5. Understanding the needs/wants of your target mate - even business-to-business purchases have a high emotional content, so imagine the impact of seeking a mate for your life.

6. Join groups that interest you, take a class, travel and talk to people when you do.

7. Be an authority – in terms of marketing, a company tries to position themselves as an authority to get publicity. In terms of a person it has the same effect. I can't even tell you how many debates I have heard about what women and men would do if they could have a night with Anderson Cooper. He is an authority figure and people are drawn to him. If you meet many single people in the course of your life who are not appropriate matches for you, don't hesitate to make a connection for them. Help out your fellow singles! Perhaps one of them will make a connection for you!

8. Greet people when it is appropriate, introduce yourself and shake hands. Make a good impression. Keep your home neat and clean. Plant flowers. Play music that will put you in a good mood when you are home, even when you are alone. Make yourself easily accessible and a pleasant person to be with... If you are in a bad mood, stay home. When you are in a good mood, make good use of it and get out there.

Just as companies do market research to better understand how they are perceived in the broader market, you too can do market research. You need to have friends you can trust to be completely honest. To do market research on yourself, you need to hear the truth about how others perceive you. Use a close friend to ask people, off the cuff, what they think of you. Remind your close friend that you want the complete truth, because you are trying to make changes in your life. People will be more likely to gossip about you to a third person than to trash you to your face. If you have chronic halitosis, then you need to hear it! If you constantly interrupt people, then you need to know that you are doing it, so you can stop and listen. If you tell long boring stories, well you probably know already that you do this, and you need to cut down on the stories, or remember to ask others about their stories.

The better understanding you have of the impression you are projecting, the better you are able to change that perception. If everyone knows you as the hawk, and going out with you becomes a challenge to meet a person and have sex, you have a lot of work to do. You need to change that perception first with your friends, and then with people you may not even know. I live in New York City, one of the largest cities in the world. Even in a city this size, people know you and have a perception of the type of person you are. If this is a bad impression, they will steer potential mates away from you, to protect their own friends. If people perceive you as a gold-digger, whether that is correct or not, they will gossip about you and keep their eligible, wealthy friends away from you. Even if you are amazing in bed, when the perception in the minds of others is that you use people for pleasure and discard them; you will be left out in the cold.

This goes the other direction as well – by that I mean, if you are a person who is always gossiping, then no one will want to open up to you, let alone date you. If you are known as a gossiper, some may be drawn to you, but are they the right people? If you go out on a date and then trash the person by telling everyone you know about some secret they entrusted to you – 1.) It will get back to them, 2.) No other man will want to go on a date and have that happen to him.

Be gracious. Be kind. Be patient and remember that old saying, "If you can't say something nice, don't say anything."

Chapter 10
Starting Conversation/Pickup

"What's your name sailor?" Yea, that line might work to start a conversation, and you can judge a man's sense of humor. If you can make a joke, without sounding too cheesy, you just might break the ice between two strangers and spark an interest. I am not saying that pick up lines that are tired should be used. But originality and humor are the best way to open up a dialogue. If it does not work, move on, do not linger where you are not wanted.

Go out with other friends to meet men. Let me warn you, the best number of women to go out together is three. That way, you can take turns going for a walk around an event or bar. This way, no one is left alone, and each one has the chance for a slow stroll, allowing a man to have the opening to approach. You can also take the opportunity to strike up a conversation with a man. Remember, that if you are not a match for a man, you will still have your friends close by. Do not arrive at an event with lots of other single females. The tendency is to talk only to the other women. A large group of women talking to each other is never a comfortable place for a single man to approach. If you know plenty of people, assemble in smaller groups and take walks between groups. On many occasions I have seen ten women seated around the edge of a patio or hotel bar. They are seated on low sofas, not at eye level, so a man cannot easily walk up and talk. Then there are so many of them lined up, a guy will be too intimidated to approach. If there are two women talking, a man can send drinks over. If you are standing, you are even more accessible. Also keep in your mind that men can smell desperation across a room. You are there to have fun with friends and if meeting a new person happens, fantastic.

Pickup lines are as old as time. Most people will simply melt if you have an original introductory line. This is because few people will take the time, or put in the energy to simply come up with an original and unique approach. Some woman can pick up a man without him even realizing he has been picked up.

Before you make any movement in the approach department, check your frame of mind. If you are miserable, you are still able to meet people, but the people you meet will be miserable as well. Like attracts like. Some miserable people can get together and make a "happy" couple. But if misery is not your normal state, please stay home. If you can fake a good mood, then do so. A good attitude is the first thing to create, and if you have any doubt, take a moment and smile in the mirror. People can hear your mood over the phone; imagine how they will pick up on your bad mood in person! If you can't smile and put yourself in a favorable disposition and be visibly convincing to yourself, then you are not going to convince others.

So turn on the charm, laugh out loud at some stupid thing you did on the way to wherever you are. Laugh at your own terrible singing in the car. Laugh at the terrible way the person next to you parked their car.

Both men and women are cautious about being approached by strangers. Keep this in mind as you approach anyone.

One good approach for women in particular is to walk past and pause to compliment the person you are interested in, then keep on walking a few steps. If they have not already noticed you, this gives them a chance to look you over. Do not go too far. Stay within earshot, so that they can respond if they are interested in speaking further. As much as people want to deny that exteriors matter, they do matter.

By complimenting the man, you have captured his attention for a brief moment and made him feel good about himself. As I may have said before, never say, "You look nice" – be more specific without being overly sexual. Make eye contact, smile, and then tell him how his suit fits his frame well. Or ask his opinion on something that will only obligate him to a short answer. "Sorry to bother you, but I've never been here before and am trying to find the ladies room." In a department store, ask a man if the color of your possible purchase looks good on you. He should be able to give a very short answer. Then you can step away… or not, if there is more conversation forthcoming.

Be thoughtful. Remember it takes a lot of courage to approach someone. Unless the person approaching is frightening you, be courteous. You can give them the brush off without being rude. He may have an attractive friend, but if he really puts you off, excuse yourself to perform some task.

Keep your expectations in check. Go out and go about your daily life without placing specific requirements on yourself: like meeting the man of your dreams in the next two months or even getting laid.

Beginning a conversation is vastly easier if you have followed my previous advice and are engaged in some common activities or volunteering. Even if you are attending the annual Fireman's Fund Ball just to meet single firemen. You can confess that bravery is something that you admire, so you are actively supporting this worthy cause.

It is easy to talk to men if you pay attention to the clues. As I stated previously, and this is very important: Men love to be complimented (but be specific and non-sexual). Say something like, "that suit really compliments your shape, you must work out," or something specific about his jewelry: a watch, a ring, cufflinks, etc. If you compliment his shoes, and they happen to be very large, that could be taken as a sexual comment – be aware and proceed with caution. If you have a foot or boot fetish, keep it to yourself for now.

Opening a conversation in a singles bar is obviously much harder than talking about horses, golf or a lecture. In big cities like New York, Boston, Chicago, and the like, we have dog runs in public parks. These can be a great place to meet others. Leave your cell phone and headphones in your purse and check out the dogs and owners around you. Ask for training tips or just ask what breed a dog happens to be – even if you already know.

A few years ago it was recommended on several talk shows and in several books and magazines that a great place to meet other single people was in the supermarket. This is still true, and I have certainly been checked out in the grocery store, long before I made it to the cashier to check out! My point in suggesting these other activities and venues is that the activity itself will not only place you in an environment with other singles, but also provide you with an opening to conversation. This gives you an introduction without having to resort to cheesy lines like some men have used for years: "What's a pretty lady like you doing in a place like this?"

To begin a conversation, be specific, be brief, and be polite.

If you see a man order a double espresso, don't just ask if he likes coffee. That is rather obvious. Think for a moment about why anyone would need that boost in caffeine. Was he working late? Was he out partying? Did his daughter cry all night? Does he have a rough day ahead? Make a comment that is funny, without being sexual or otherwise offensive. Women are more emotionally based creatures than men, or at least more in touch with their emotions. Keep this in mind and get your mind into the emotion of why he is having that double espresso. Pay attention to how he is dressed, what he is carrying, did he order food as well.

Focus on the man in front of you and listen to what he has to say. Make him feel like he is the only person in the room, and he will notice.

Chivalry is not dead, it's in a coma, so sometimes men have to be coaxed into it. Women do not want to be treated as equals; woman want to be treated BETTER. And I mean better than a he treats his buddies. Most women want a door opened and a chair pulled out. If he was not raised with manners, they can be learned. There are books and even coaches. You can be casual and still have manners. As a woman, do not always expect a man to pick up the tab or go fetch a drink at the bar during a party. He will appreciate that you are paying attention.

I know one woman who recently asked me about how to resolve the problem of dating a man who makes less than half her salary. She is beautiful, tall, poised and happens to make a great living. She is intimidating for most men on so many levels. I suggested that she make some inexpensive suggestions for things to do, where he can afford to pay. Then on other occasions they can go to a place that is a bit more expensive. She can now say, "You paid last time, please let me get this." Or she can insist, "Hey, you got the last time, it's my turn." Let the man know that you had such a great time on the last date that you also want to contribute. Men have fragile egos when it comes to money issues. Be aware and don't trample them when they are not the Rockefellers.

Getting back to meeting new people, if you want to breaking into a pack to talk to someone: Send a round of drinks (yes cheapskate, the whole pack gets a round). This is the most effective way to open up a pack to having you join. This is not taboo for women to do – but it is situational. Be careful that the whole pack of guys does not expect something more for their free drink.

Another method is to stand close and listen attentively. At the right pause in the conversation, ask a question of the person speaking, about whatever they have been saying. Once you are answered, you become part of the conversation.

Approaching a person who is alone can be as easy as asking a general question, like: "How are you doing this evening?" From this you will get an idea of the level of interest; if the answer is multiple words, then chances are better that they are open to conversation. Do not stand or sit too close. Do not be too aggressive – otherwise you come off as an "easy" woman.

Ask something like, "What brings you out this evening?" Talk for a few minutes and then excuse yourself. Gauge whether they want you to return or not by their comments, body language or sometimes even an offer to wait for you. The act of leaving after a few minutes is very key here. This allows the other person to have a taste of your personality and a chance to process it in their brain. Stepping away like this can be a very hard thing to learn. Once you are engaged and excited about talking, it can be hard to break away. If you truly feel that staying is important, go with your instincts and don't leave. Every situation is different. But you may be surprised at how even a few moments away can make them want to talk to you more.

Phone number protocol

This is a delicate subject for a lot of people. You have to feel whether it will be perceived in the right way. If you don't feel like your intentions will be taken as honorable, don't give your number and don't ask for one. If you know someone in common, you can always ask later if the person you liked - felt the same about you. If there is a mutual attraction, then numbers can be exchanged. If however you feel that your intention will be made more clear by offering rather than asking for a phone number, then give it. Clearly, if your intention is a quick sexual encounter, then the man will probably figure that out. I have had very aggressive women come on to me and even whisper what they wanted to do with me, once they got me home. But if your intention is an actual date, then make it clear and give a date and time that will be best for him to call – or set a meeting date and time right then and there. If the attraction is mutual, there is nothing wrong with saying something like, "I know you like the theater from what you said earlier, I happen to have a connection and would love for you to join me to see a show next week." This makes it clear that your intention is a date. This also makes it clear that you were listening to their interests (you didn't ask them to a tractor pull, because you actually heard that they did that last week and hated it). By saying that you "have a connection" you have lessoned the impact on your ego if the person declines your invitation. It is an open offer, but it is specific enough that should the other person decline without offering an alternative, then you have been let down easily. If you are declined without them offering an alternative, LET IT GO. You do not want to press the issue with a person who is not interested. Likewise, if someone asks you out and you are interested, but not available – DO offer an alternative date or time to meet. This will make it clear that you are interested in getting to know them, and are not giving them the brush off.

First impressions are made in two seconds as I have said before. Make sure that you are ready for that, be polite and remember the looser you meet tonight could be the best friend of Prince Charming...

Attitude – Be upbeat and positive without being fake. If you are out to meet a new person, you don't want to spill your guts about all your problems with work or family! If things work out, there is plenty of time to draw them into your well of self-pity and misery. If they don't work out, why bring down everyone you meet? Ok, I'm being overly harsh to make a point. The reality is that if you have had a bad day, sometimes going out can cheer you up. But don't go into details of your unhappiness. You are out to let go of your stress and enjoy yourself. If the current day is not going well, talk about where you are going in life and what your plans are for the future. If you have no plans, make some up! Also keep in mind that if you are prone to spilling your guts when meeting someone and thus scaring them off, maybe you need to change course and become a listener. People love a listener. This is an effective method of endearing people to you, especially men.

Remember presence, awareness, body language and tonality – if you are the timid wallflower, fine, but you leave yourself open to being the prey of trolls. If you know how to dismiss the trolls and play the timid role well and long enough, you can entice the hottie into your web, and you have a skill I never mastered. Be aware of what signals you are giving. Practice going out a few times and being super aware of what you are doing. Take notes if you want. This is really a practice. After two or three times of going out and consciously realizing your patterns, you can learn to go with what is comfortable, but you will be more aware of what to avoid. You went out 3 times and were the wallflower the whole time. You promise yourself next time to bring a friend, so you have someone to talk to and hopefully make it easier to transition into speaking with others. If you are the extrovert, you will learn to be aware of when that behavior will work best, and when it will put people off, and you need to tone it down. Unless you live in a small town, do not frequent the same place too often. You don't want people to know all of your business. You want to have an air of mystery about you. People who recognize you should be able to say, "We haven't seen you for a while, where have you been?"

You need to be able to respond with an answer other than, "Alone on my sofa with the cat and a pint of Ben & Jerry's." You need to be able to say that you have been out on dates or out doing something interesting - from a movie to travel, taking a class, something!

Handshakes

When you are being introduced it is customary to shake hands. Women in particular give the limp-dishrag handshake. This says to a man that you are to be considered as wimpy, passive, or even submissive. With some women, this is the role they want to project. They want a man to be an alpha male and take a more dominant role. If you do not want to project this, if you as a woman want to be more equal, you shake hands full hand and firm. The webs of your hands should touch.

If you are introducing yourself in a casual setting, use only your first name. Women may remain seated when being introduced to a standing person, but if it seems that everyone else is standing, go with it and stand. If you have a unique name or your name has a unique spelling, take the 2 seconds to spell it or clarify. If someone is introduced to you with an unusual name (like Blaise), never make a joke at his or her expense. It is rude and can be hurtful. The most common response to my name is: "You mean like Blazing Saddles." Or something like, "Is that your 'real' name or a porn name?" Okay, that was funny the first 100 times. Now that I am passed the 1000th time, I am no longer amused. Such people are quickly dismissed as simpletons. If someone has the intelligence to ask, "Like Blaise Pascal?" then I am impressed. Mostly, it is much nicer to just say, "That is an interesting name, what is the origin?" You will have complimented them and provided a point of conversation. Most people with a unique name will have quite a few stories.

Chapter 11
Preparing for a First Date/Blind Date

Where do you wanna go? I don't know, where do you wanna go? I don't know, where do you wanna go? Stop that!

Men often do not take the initiative when it comes to planning the date. If have you caught yourself saying, "I don't know" or "Whatever you'd like" when planning a date, there is a problem. When a man calls to ask a woman out, the best approach is for him to give a few fun and creative date options and ask her to pick one. But as a woman, know that all men are not so organized. So you should have some options in your own mind. Think of things you enjoy and that a man would enjoy doing as well. Most straight men will not want to go shoe shopping with you. That's for your gay friends. If you like the theater, some men will love seeing a live show. If you love horseback riding, make a note of the nearest stables and use that as a suggestion of something different to do.

Don't be afraid to make suggestions. Some women never speak up and they end up being miserable at the Monster Truck rally. Speak up, you want to have a good time as well as get to know this new person.

Have the initiative to approach your date with ideas, passion and interest. You can be flirty and forward, letting him know it's okay for him to kiss you or say how amazing you think he looks (remember to be specific).

As a woman, you should expect men to be chivalrous, open the doors, hold your chair, and pick up the check. He should lift up off his chair when you get up to go to the bathroom and then get up and help you with you chair when you return. If that does not happen but is important to you, he can learn. If this is not important to you, no problem. If he cannot or will not learn, move on.

Many women want a bad boy-type man. Then they go about changing him and are surprised when he treats them poorly. Some men are not worth your time, even when they have an animal magnetism you seek. A good man will have the raw materials and interest in pleasing you (and you in pleasing him), that you both can hone and refine each other into the perfect match. Yes opening doors, pulling out chairs and the like are fantastic, but after a while you want to see the real him. If this is really him, then fine, but if it is not yet, he may be chivalrous in other ways that are in line with what you see as the ideal man/mate, and you have hit the jackpot.

Keys to a successful first date:
- Make sure you are up on the latest news or have something to discuss.
- Dress appropriately. When in doubt, overdress.
- Turn off the cell phone during the date (unless you have children). A ringing cell phone tells your date that you're not serious about them.
- Always make eye contact with the person to whom you are speaking.
- Bring dental supplies with you. I once ordered a roast beef and there was a string of meat stuck in my teeth. I would've excused myself

to the bathroom to fix it, but I hadn't brought my floss with me. So I sat there, not listening and going crazy. Now if I have enough pockets (coat, etc) I bring mints, gum, spray, floss, everything. Seriously

- You've got to distinguish yourself from the pack. You do this by being engaging and offering a potential mate something more than others.

- At the conclusion of the date, Always thank him (Yes, even if you paid). Shake hands or kiss on the cheek. You have the power here to make it clear if something more may be acceptable. As a woman, you are in control here, take control and let the guy know whether a kiss on the lips is acceptable.

When it comes to blind or Internet dating, don't waste too much time emailing or calling back and forth. Once you like the person from the initial conversation, meet up (in a public place)! The guy may have the voice of Luther Vandros and the body of Barney Rubble. He may be thinking you have the face of Halle Barry, but have the personality of Cruella DeVille.

If you did not have a good time, never say you will call. Do not even bring up the subject. If the other person brings it up and wants a second date, be diplomatic but honest. Okay, if you can't be honest, at least do not give the impression that you will be calling anytime soon. Acting like you plan to follow up with another date, when you're not, bothers most men. Never underestimate the way word travels about you not keeping your word. Men have fragile egos, but would still rather you end a date that was not a match by saying, "It was nice to meet you. Have a good night." Never act like you plan to follow up if you have no such intention. If you go out more than a few times and feel no romantic connection, be honest. Let the man know that while you enjoy his company, you do not feel a romantic connection. If you are afraid to say it in person, say it in an email or a text message. Do NOT say it to one of his friends. No one wants to hear that kind of information from a third party. No one wants others to know that a relationship is not going anywhere, before they themselves know. Remember that communication is usually the way to go with a man. Men are less likely to share their emotional hurt and pain, but we DO feel it. No one wants to have their ego or their hopes crushed.

If you are having a great time on your date, there are subtle ways to let the other person know that you are interested in more. Body language tells a lot about what you are feeling. Smile and laugh when he says something funny. This may sound like common sense, but some people are so uptight on a date (blind date or otherwise) that they feel self-conscious and do not let out a good laugh. If you feel a connection, relax and let him know by giving a good laugh, or a smile.

When you are feeling a connection, lean in to the conversation. Leaning away from a person is the body language signal that you are pulling away from them. Leaning toward him gives the body language signal that you are engaged in the conversation, and want to be closer to him, literally and figuratively. So lean in and make eye contact.

If your date brings up a topic that is something you really love, respond with questions so you can become more involved in that topic. Asking questions when your date says something related to an area of your interest is the best way to show him that you are listening. This will also bring you into a deeper conversation.

Remember to keep your body language open as you open up in the conversation. Crossing your arms, your legs or even your hands is a sign that you are inaccessible and closed off. If you see yourself doing this, recognize that perhaps the conversation has become too personal. You can either uncross your body and go ahead and open up, or simply change the subject. If you are genuinely interested, you want to be able to invite the date into your personal space. This may be as simple as sitting on two connected sides of a square, dining table, instead of across from each other. You may lock your pinky fingers on the armrest in a movie theater, instead of holding hands. Subtle signals can send very strong messages. There is an art to courting. Simply sitting on the front porch and talking is a great way to get to know each other.

Chapter 12
Further Dates

If you want to go on several dates, give some indication to the guy. If he is not asking, you can ask! Don't stand on some old tradition and let a great guy who may be a little timid, get away.

Go out and see how things go. In your mind you will be interviewing him, and he will be interviewing you. My first priority in a new dating situation after looks (Yea, I admit it) is a sense of humor. If the person can make you smile or even laugh, then they are miles ahead of others in terms of relationship material. Several years ago, I was rushed to the emergency room in agony so bad I was praying for death. What allowed me to escape the pain in my body was not the painkillers, but the funny stories from life and travel that I could recall from years of a happy relationship.

Obviously, you cannot be laughing all the time, but having someone around who can make you smile, laugh, think, someone who listens when you speak and does little things to make you happy - will go a long way toward creating a happy relationship. You will also be able to tell after a few long dates, whether you have listened to this person you have met. You will see whether you have made mental notes of things they love: from favorite foods, to how they take their coffee, to whether they are close to their family. When you feel the urge to do little things to make him happy, and you see him doing little things for you, or remembering your stories and details about things you have said, then he is worth getting to know even better.

Generally women will be the ones to begin a discussion about the relationship. Women are often conditioned to clarify the position and direction of a relationship from time to time. Most men are oblivious, at least on the outside. Men frequently want to work things out in their minds before they say anything, whereas women want to talk everything out.

When you initiate a discussion of your relationship and the direction it is taking, bear in mind that men are not comfortable with the unknown and may be concerned that you will end up in tears. Please do not ambush a man and make him feel like he is going to the principal's office or being pulled over for speeding. To ease into such a talk, start with something positive, work in the concern, and end with something positive. If you want to know if a new man views you as marriage material, don't say: "Hey, am I your girlfriend or what?" You might fair better with: "I really like you a lot. I would love for you to meet my family and friends. We've been having so much fun, I hope they like you!"

This is a subtle way of saying, "Hey dude, I like you and I want to introduce you around as my new boyfriend." But the topic will be much easier for him to digest than simply demanding a clear direction of where he thinks things are going. If the idea of being identified as your boyfriend to your family and friends scares him off, then you have your answer and need to move on.

If you want to broach the subject of moving in with him after you have been dating for a while, try "I think we have an amazing relationship, and I'm ready to take the next step and move in together. Think of how much fun we'd have living under the same roof!" A man will first think of sex all the time, while you are thinking about nesting. Keep that in mind, but don't say it unless you both have the sense of humor that can handle it. Let me say, I still believe that marriage is preferable to just living together. I also believe that you should date a while before marriage.

When dating a man, you also have to pull back once in while. If you are too available, he will take you for granted and begin to loose interest. He will still love you, but like Christmas morning when you were a child, you want to play with all the new toys, not the ones you have loved and played with all year long. Pull back once in while and then do something new and different. This can be as simple as making a picnic lunch and going to the park, or hopping in the shower with him and scrubbing his back.

Part of the interplay in a relationship is the lure and the chase. If either of you is too available, then you run the risk of your interest in each other diminishing over time. This is true not just when dating, but even after marriage. When you want a man to stay interested after a few dates, you have to sometimes have other plans. This does not mean canceling without notice or saying "no" to a date with him. I mean that you sometimes have to see your friends without him. When he asks you out for your 3rd or 5th date, say you are busy. Don't stop there, propose an alternative day, so he knows you do want to see him, but that you have a full life and you are going to try to blend him into it. This leaves a man wanting more. All men have a bit of the hunter in them; give him a reason to chase.

You may want to come up with a few things to gauge his willingness to chase. Be like a cat: play with your food before you eat it.

Change something he really likes about you and make it obvious. For instance if he likes for you to not wear perfume... wear it. If he likes your hair long, shorten it a little... it will grow back. If he likes a certain color of lipstick, wear it long enough for him to get use to it and then change it drastically. If your X liked you to wear your hair up, make sure your new boyfriend knows that and wear it up, especially if your new man likes to see your hair down. If he notices and comments on these things then the chase is on. Give him the satisfaction of you conditioning yourself to his needs, but know it is you that is doing the conditioning, stop wearing the perfume, let your hair grow back, wear the lipstick he likes, or wear your hair down just like he likes it.

Look at it this way, if you noticed him trimming his body hair out of the blue for no reason what would you think... now you are doing the chasing.

If he likes to see you wearing heels, then wear them sparingly. But when you do wear them, cross your legs and make sure he notices those heels!

Sometimes, let his call or text go unanswered for a while. Wait a few hours before getting back to him. He will wonder what you were doing, and feel drawn into you.

All relationships are an interplay of interests, emotions, intellect and raw lust. Keeping someone interested and excited by you is work, but it is fulfilling and both of you will be more eager to share time and blend into each others lives.

If a man tells you that he is not ready for a relationship, take his word for it. Men really do hate to disappoint women, so if he has summoned the courage to actually say the words, and tell you that he's not ready for a relationship, he is serious. There could be a variety of explanations for his position (he has commitment issues, he wants to meet other people, he doesn't see you as girlfriend material). The point is the same regardless: He does not feel the desire to be your boyfriend: End of story. And no, he won't change his mind when he gets to know you a little better. When a man decides how he views a woman in his life, it is hard to break out of that thinking. If you don't walk away after he has told you this, then you are telling him you are okay with a casual, non-exclusive relationship. He will see you as a buddy and a booty-call.

Communication

During my preparation for this book I was having a discussion with several women at once. Another woman overheard part of the conversation and the lovely Karyn joined us. She said she had something to confess, and I blurted out "'of course you do!" It was quite a funny moment.

Karyn had cut and paste using her phone from a text she received from one man, then sent it to another with some changes. What she did not realize was that it appeared on the second man's screen in a different color and when he rolled over it, he was able to see the original person's name and the date it was sent. Here she is... an original, witty, pretty and funny girl, and now the guy may be thinking she doesn't have her own material. She does have her own material, but she just wasn't using it. Being "original" is an essential part of sex appeal.

Picasso said: "Good artists copy, great artists steal." But you should never appear to be a hack. If your approach lacks originality and individuality... you may loose out. It is a person's unique way of being, looking at things, that catches one's counterpart, hook, line and sinker.

Chapter 13
Children/Blending Families

There are many things to consider in dating. But at a certain age, children are something that must be considered. If dating someone with no children is very important to you, remember you are narrowing the field of eligible people. Remember also that the ones with kids are often (not always) a little more broken in. They understand how to share their lives with another. They may also come with a lot of baggage. Like anything, it is a gamble and you have to get a feeling for whether it will work in a matter of a date or two, maybe three.

One of the most important factors in dating a person with children is recognizing what your place is in the family dynamic. Even though you are just dating, there are still emotions involved, and you have to know ahead of time that things can be volatile. This is even truer if there is an ex-spouse involved.

Start with talking to the man you want to date or have started dating. Learn what the involvement level is of the other parent of the children. Remember that hostility from a second parent can influence children a great deal and can damage a relationship that could actually be a good fit. Make sure that you are always a friend first to the children, regardless of the age. Once you have built and gained trust from them, then and only then will they listen and learn from you as an authority. This may not happen in the first week after meeting them, or even the first month.

If all goes well, you can build into becoming an authority to listen to and from whom they can learn. DO NOT start off a dating relationship functioning as the disciplinarian of someone else's children. You will be setting yourself up for being hated by the children. The parent who is not present when you are trying to provide the discipline may also challenge you.

When I say this – it is based on my own experience. My own father moved his girlfriend in to our home three weeks after my mother died. She had no experience with caring for children, and tried to obliterate the memory of our mother by removing all photos of her, rearranging all the furniture and banning us from seeing our maternal grandparents with whom we had spent at least one weekend a month since birth.

Dating a person with children is a delicate balance and you have to befriend the kids first. Talk to the person you are dating and ease into spending time with the children together. One of my closest friends recommends at least a month of dating and I have heard others say up to 6 months. I think that you will know within a month if the guy is someone you want to continue seeing. So I think a month or so is a good time frame. Pick a restaurant, where the kids will have fun. Arrive separately, do not place any pressure on the children, but let them casually know you are meeting up with a friend. You can even run into each other casually and see if your children and the person and/or their children can get along. Putting pressure on them to be friends immediately will sometimes work against you.

Leave the rough stuff like discipline or correcting behavior to their actual parent. Now I'm not saying that if the child is five years old and running around screaming in a restaurant that you have to deal with it. First, you would need to decide if a person who allows that sort of behavior in his child is someone you want. Second you have to see how they deal with such a situation. I am a proponent of disciplining children and being consistent in that discipline. You cannot allow a child to misbehave in public because you don't want to be seen correcting them. I am also not one to follow those people who never say "no" to children. Children need to hear "NO" and be able to handle it. When they reach adulthood they will hear "no" quite often. They need to learn how to either accept it, or find creative ways around it.

When you are the person with the children and are dating someone without children, you have to know when your kids are ready. Generally, your child does not need to know the details of your dating life, or your online dating activity. When you have older children, high school age or older, they are more likely to be able to understand and handle information about your love life. However, it's important that you see serious long-term potential before you integrate the man you're dating into your family.

Remember that your child did not choose to be in their situation; and after going through a divorce or the loss of a parent, stability is important for her or him. Refer to your new date as a 'friend' until you are certain that the relationship is something more.

If you have children and are creating an online profile, spend less only a few lines of your profile talking about your child or children. People understand that being a Mom is an important part of your life, and you should mention this in the profile. I recommend that you spend a few lines talking about your favorite activities with your child and maybe what you love about being a parent. Then move on to other aspects of you. There should be more interests and facets to your identity than being a Mom. So find the balance when you're writing your online profile.

Always include simple photos of yourself - a close up and one full-body shot works best online. If you are in particularly good shape, you may want to include a photo at the beach or by the pool. But remember that if you are heavy, you are no less attractive and may want to include something along the same lines. I know one friend who is a Big Buxom Woman (BBW) with a 5'7" 370 lbs frame and a 56i chest. She was too shy about her weight to include any photo showing her body below the shoulders in a profile. She is a BIG girl, but she has a great figure. Without seeing a full body photo, you would never know how hot she is.

If you want to include a photo of your child in your profile, that's fine too - just remember that the Internet attracts predators. For this reason, you may not want to post a shot that shows a clear view of your child's face or advertises too much personal or contact information. Keep it simple. Remember that the profile is about YOU and your child is only one aspect of who you are.

Chapter 14
Interracial/Intercultural Dating

Truly, interracial marriage is much less of an issue these days, than it was before the court case: Loving vs. Virginia made it legal. But this does not mean that there are not challenges. Dating someone with a different background, be it economic, social, locale, or other customs, will always pose problems and challenges. Most important is the need to respect the other person's culture. True, you may have been raised in the same town and attended the same schools. But when you date a person with a different background, they will have different experiences, even in the same environment.

For example, when a very tall person is coming to visit your home, you might go around and dust all the upper shelves, the tops of the floor lamps, the tops of the picture frames, etc. You know that a person over 6'6" is much more likely to be looking down at these things, and see that you are not as neat as others might think. This tall person will see your home with an entirely different perspective than a 5'2" person – even though all the things in the room are in the same places, and the conversation is the same. Its not the same as experiencing what it is like to be another race, but try this exercise:

> To get a feel for this different perspective, take a moment and put a chair in the center of your living room. Stand on it and see how different your room feels. Do the same in your bathroom or dining room. You might even try doing this at your front door, to see what they will see, when they walk into your

home. Unless you are in the range of 6'6",
you are bound to notice differences in how
your home appears.

Now try this exercise from the perspective of
a 5'2" person, from the same locations around
your home. You will notice different things.
Perhaps at 6'6", you noticed that the picture
frames needed to be wiped down. At 5'2"
you noticed that there are smudges on your
mirrors or sliding glass doors. These are just
minor differences, but they give you a better
understanding of how easily perspective can
be altered. You can understand how
differently you see the world when you are a
different race and how differently people see
you.

Now try to imagine you are Asian and think about
how your day might be different. If you were from
Mexico or Brazil, how different would your daily
routine be from what it is now? What different foods
would you eat in the course of your day? Where
would you buy your clothes? Would you listen to
Country music? Would it be music from Bollywood
in India? How different would your day be, and how
differently would you be treated if you were a Seik
and wore a turban whenever you left the house?
What would the reaction to you be, if you walked
into your office in a burka or a Hebrew prayer shawl?
Your experience of the same places and events would
be completely altered.

When you are the only white person in an all-black
church, you can understand what your date might
feel, as a black person in an all-white restaurant.

Neither of these experiences is good or bad, they are just different and need to be understood.

I am not claiming that any culture is superior to another.

Part of the purpose of the exercise was to get you to see things from a different point of view. Remember though that coming from a different race or culture, means that you are not just looking around from a different angle. Other people are also looking back at you from a different perspective. Different races of people and different classes of people will be treated in completely different manners in the same environment. Two white people pulling up to the valet at a Ritz Carlton might seem perfectly equal. However, if one is dressed in a suit, and steps out of a brand new Lamborghini, they will be treated differently from the person stepping out of a 10 year old, dented and dirty pick up truck. The one with the beat up truck may be worth millions. The person in the brand new Lamborghini may be in debt to the eyeballs. They may be treated equally well, or they may not. It could even be the same person, on two different days, but they will generally not be perceived as the same.

How you are treated is based on many factors. Since I am white, I have had issues when I dated someone who was not white, both from the white community and from the community of the person I was seeing. Not all, but some Black Americans have a problem with a Black American dating a white American. Oddly enough, in England and Scandinavia, I never had any white person say anything to me when I was on a date with a black person. The odd part is going out where there are single people and one or the other of us was ignored, like we did not exist. Be prepared for the reactions of others, and feel free to laugh about them.

As another exercise, try shopping for food in a grocery that caters specifically to the Hispanic market, or to the Asian market. If you are from one of these backgrounds, go to a store in a mostly black or mostly white area, and see the different foods available. Take notice of how you are treated compared to others around you. I am white, so when I shop in the stores that cater to the Hispanic buyer, I am treated differently. I am delighted to find three or four different brands of Mole (Mexican, spicy, cocoa-based sauce). These are the kinds of experiences that you and your partner will go through, when you date a person of a different race or culture.

Food is another important part of racial/cultural mix. You will have to learn to like each other's ethnic or even regional foods (or at least tolerate them). I have heard stories from a friend, about what a great Italian cook his mother is, even though she is Irish. She took the effort of spending time in the kitchen with her future mother-in-law, learning how to prepare the favorite Italian dishes of her fiancée.

I know of another couple that met on vacation in France. He was from an island culture and she was from a bustling city. She was from Spain and was fluent in Spanish and French. The man she met was from Portugal; he spoke Portuguese and French. When they married, they spoke French to each other and gradually learned each other's native tongue. They taught each other the cooking from their respective cultures. Later this same couple moved to the United States and both had to learn English. They learned to embrace the cultural differences and taught their daughter to be part of the US culture, while honoring her multicultural background.

Families can be against you beginning a life with a man from a different racial, ethnic or social background. The family influence can be a huge factor depending on the power of their authority over your man. One man I interviewed was dating a woman of mixed race for months and was informed by her that she was Puerto Rican and Castilian from Spain. In reality, she was the daughter of a black American and a Castilian Spaniard. She had such internalized racism that she did not want to even admit that she was half-black. Her own father was extremely racist and seemed to be like the black version of the television character: Archie Bunker. This kind of racism can become a part of your relationship. Remember that even your grandparents will become involved, if they feel strongly about the union.

Statistically each of your families will be less likely to be involved in the lives of your children if your children do not look like them. Some families will be the exception and will be more concerned about making sure the child has all their fingers and toes. But be prepared to handle the racism as a couple, and to support each other when instances occur.

You will often have trouble getting other families to socialize with you, including other parents. There is a strong undercurrent of racism in the US, where people will be friendly on the baseball fields while watching their children, but will not include you and your mixed race family in other outings or events. Do not let that stop you from inviting them and their children to parties for your own family. Break down these walls.

One of the men I interviewed talked about his beautiful Brazilian wife and this odd problem she has encountered. Even at their church or on the game field with her daughter, she has had other mothers assume she was a mail-order bride! The other mothers tried to get her to leave her devoted husband and take half of everything they own together. She says she has come home in tears after these encounters. Realize that people will get into your business and assume many things. Life will be much harder in a blended-race marriage, but if you truly love each other, you can weather the storms. The film, "Guess Whose Coming to Dinner" was filmed in 1967 about a white young woman who falls in love with a widowed black man (portrayed by Sydney Poitier). It was a landmark film that was so disturbing to the American psyche that it was not even shown in theaters in the Deep South. Forty years later, that racism has diminished, but still persists. Be ready and able to cope and talk openly with your partner. This same Brazilian friend talks about how sad the US couples seem to her, in that they are not united. The women seem to want a rich husband and the men want a trophy wife. The women sit on the sidelines at their children's athletic games and talk badly with each other about their husbands. When they asked her what complaints she had, she said, "He's perfect. I have minimal expectations, because you never know what you are getting into. I expect him not to cheat. If he cleans the house, that is a bonus. If he washes the clothes and takes care of the kids, I am happy. We balance each other."

Her husband says, "I put my God first, my wife second and my kids third. That's how I run my life." This is not a preachy, overly religious man, this is a simple guy who happens to love his wife and believes that honoring her, and their relationship is one of his top priorities. He says, "I don't make the final decisions, we make the final decisions together." He does not even consider their racial difference to be significant.

Chapter 15
Dating After Death of a Partner

Dating after the loss of your partner-in-life has to be the most challenging moment in terms of the dating world. There is no other time when a person has to actually deal with the feeling that you are betraying the one you love and there is nothing you can do about it.

Part of the healing process after loosing a loved one is recognizing that you are still alive, and want companionship. Clearly, dating after the loss of a partner is not for everyone. Many people live out the rest of their lives alone and are okay with that. But for many other people, simply being alone is not an option. To some singles, a widow or widower is the perfect mate. As a widow, you have been through all the ups and downs of a relationship and stuck it out. You are already broken-in, like a good pair of gloves or jeans. You know what to expect, how to behave and when to do whatever needs to be done for your man and your relationship.

You have to prepare yourself for the feelings of jealously and betrayal you will feel the first time you go out with a new man after your loss.

Before you embark on dating after the loss of your husband, talk openly with a family member or close friend. Whether you have good or bad things to say, talk out all the problems you and your former husband had in the relationship. You want to let out all the good, the bad and the ugly. Talk about the hardest of times, the worst sleepless nights. You may even want to record the conversations for writing of a book or simply as an oral family history.

Then I want you to talk again with the same person if possible, and tell the stories of love with your lost husband. Tell the stories of tenderness, the little things that made you happy together. Tell them about the exciting big things you did, and the moments when you had the flu and the love you felt as he cared for you. I want you to get all of the talk about your partner out, so that when it comes time to date again, you are able to talk about other topics that have nothing to do with the partner you have lost.

It will be a challenge for you to keep the conversation from drifting to times your shared with the love you have lost, but you will recall such times with love and be able to say, "we went to Catalina Island once and it was beautiful, let me tell you about the trip." This will allow you to honor the one you continue to love but have lost, by recalling that he was present with you on a trip. But then focus on the story you want to tell about your travels. This is a healthy way to incorporate him, without the lost one being the dominant factor of the conversation.

You will need to honor the man who shared your life for many years. You also do not want to burden the new man with the job of trying to live up to the perfect image of a lost loved one. As time passes – you will heal.

As I have said at other times, you never really get over the death of a truly close person in your life; you just learn to live with them in your heart, instead of in your sight. This is doubly true of a spouse.

If you are strong enough to have read through this and recalled the bad times, the fights and devastating moments, then you will be fine. You will also look back on the triumphs, the celebrations, the laughter and joy you have shared. Smile for the good times and bring that joy into your life as you begin dating again. Most husbands would want their wife to go on and be happy.

Joy, Bursting Out
Through despair there is hope,
Through doubt, there is trust,
Through misery, there is joy.

I long for laughter's return,
and the moment I hear that
child-like giggle, only to
realize it is my own joy, bursting out.[iv]

Chapter 16
Dating After Divorce

Pardon me while I sweep away the ashes of my ex husbands clothes… I burned them.

Divorces can be smooth or they can be quite ugly. The most important thing to remember is that you are a whole person, with or without your partner. You may have set off on the road together, but you each reached different destinations or crossroads on your journey. Now you have parted, and you have to know in your heart that you are a complete person. One friend I know took over a year before dating again. He had to rediscover himself. He had allowed his wife to rewrite who he was. In order to recover, he had to go back to the original self. Don't go through the "I have lost something and I have to replace it." Heal yourself first, before you try to find something to replace the things you have lost. Reconnecting with old friends can often help you rebuild the traits about yourself that you loved. You have to achieve a positive self-worth and be whole, before you can effectively move on.

If you have children, work to keep your negative feelings for your ex-husband from affecting your relationship with your kids. Even if your ex was a "low down dirty dog," your children do not need to hear you talking badly about him all the time. You have moved on by getting a divorce. So now the healing and self-discovery begins.

With that said, dating after divorce is where you have healed your heart to the point that you are ready to at least test the waters of meeting others. You do not need to jump in and get remarried immediately. You must begin the process knowing that it is all right to date men, as you are adjusting to being single again. Be clear with the men you date. Let them know you are still healing and they will understand. Do not expect or even consider remarriage until you can HONESTLY say that you have healed, and say it aloud to yourself and your friends (without them laughing).

Part of the difficulty for many people in dating after a divorce is getting to the point where you feel you are worthy of love. Often the divorce leaves one or both partners with a feeling of failure. But what you have to discover within yourself is that even though one relationship did not succeed, you as a person will continue and CAN succeed.

Think back for a moment about the little arguments you had in grade school that led to you not talking to a friend for weeks. If you can recall, there is a lesson that you learned back in that more simple time. The lesson is that you can survive separation from someone. You thought they were so close that they were a part of you. In grade school, friendships are often one's whole world. You survived the separating at this most critical time in your early life, even though you may have forgotten it as an adult. The lesson is still there. As an adult, you can now draw on the feeling of triumph you felt at having freed yourself from dependence on another. Looking back on the lessons of your childhood can help you see across the bridge from separation, to the happiness you once had and will achieve again as a single, but complete person.

When divorce is a relief, you still need to mend afterward. The pain of the relationship and the drama in your life has come to a close. You may feel a tremendous burden has been lifted, but you will still need to time to heal. You have to get your bearings as a single person. One of the biggest aspects of a divorce that is rarely discussed in courtrooms is who gets the friends you have made together. There is no mechanism to work out the custody of the list of friendships you have created and nurtured together. Figuring out who gets each friend after the divorce will also determine what support network you will have in the weeks, months and years to come.

Mostly, your family will stick by you. Also the friendships that you had prior to your relationship will mostly stay with you. However, if you have not maintained these friendships over the course of the marriage, then you may be starting from scratch.

It will help a great deal, for most people, to have a network of friends and family around and available, as you transition into your new life. Most people will want an ear to listen to them when they begin the dating process. You will need that ear as well, when you want to complain or rejoice about other aspects of your new life. If you have been married for a while, you have generally become accustomed to having a person there to talk, day or night. It will be hard to live without this sounding board and comfort zone.

When you meet new people, you should generally avoid putting them into this category too soon. It may scare people off if you start confiding too many of your darkest secrets and wildest dreams too early in the relationship. You will probably not want to call up the person you just spent time with on a date, to criticize them. You need a friend to do that. You may want a friend to look at your wardrobe and your home and give you honest feedback about how you can make it date-friendly. There should not be altars of devotion to your ex. By this I mean that photos of your ex should not grace the walls and their personal touches no longer need to be part of your new décor. If you have children, you may want to have them keep a photo of your ex in their room, since it is still their parent. But take down group photos and portraits of the ex from the walls of public areas of your home. They will make any new paramour feel uncomfortable and left out.

I suggest that divorced people follow the same exercise I discussed in Chapter 15, Dating After The Death of a Partner. As I said there, sit down with a friend (or even a therapist) and spill your guts about all the bad things in the relationship. Once you have let out the bad, go back. This time take notes or even record as you talk about all the good times. Discuss how you met, what drew you in to marry him; what made you most happy during the marriage. Then try to let it all go.

You need to adjust to the single life again. However, like men, women should date several people and enjoy your new independence. Go on dates with various types of men, become familiar with their personalities and their differences from you. See what makes them alike or different from each other. During this dating period, see what type of guy is most attractive to you in ways beyond sexual

126

attraction or your blueprint of marriage material. Once you have begun to see yourself as a whole person, healed mentally from the divorce, you will have the perspective to sort through the personality traits. You will have a better idea of what you want to avoid and what you truly seek in a new relationship.

Chapter 17
Age Differences

Be prepared to laugh off the comments like "Whoa Daddy!" or "Craddle robber". I met a woman recently who loves younger men. She is in her forties and is dating a handsome man in his mid-20s. Her response to others when they say something about the age disparity is simple: "If you can't find a good man out there, raise one of your own."

Dating is about finding common ground. Dating yourself would be boring, mostly because you already know everything about yourself, so conversation would not exist, unless you have multiple personalities! Age differences can hinder or enhance a relationship, depending upon how well the couple handle themselves. A difference in age is another aspect of the relationship and is as relevant or as irrelevant as your difference in height. A few years, to a few decades, the disparity in age can provide conversation points and learning experiences on both sides. The older person will not always be the teacher, and needs to be prepared and open to learning a few new things along the way.

Likewise, the younger person should expect to learn, and to listen to stories. The younger person should also be prepared with new insights, and both must be open to learning new things and growing, together.

When I was 22 years old, I dated someone who was 44 years old. After a few weeks, I had to break it off. The older person was not mature enough for me. I had more life experience and handled myself better in business and personal situations than this person who was double my age!

On another occasion, I spent a whole-day date with someone 10 or 12 years older. This was an online meeting, so I knew there was an age difference.

I tend to like athletic builds, but this person was carrying much more fat on their body and was much less active than I was led to believe. If I had been told the honest truth about the body type, I would not have been surprised and would not have felt a bit betrayed. Again, honesty is very important, especially in online dating. Since this was an online meeting, I had only seen photographs and we did not know anyone in common. We met at a restaurant then left my car behind. When I opened the door to get into her car, the trash had to be cleared from the seat before I could sit down. Here was another red flag in my mind, which I was gracious enough to ignore. I wanted to have a good time and I set my preconceived notions aside for a while.

After the date, we exchanged emails. I asked how the date went and was shocked by the answer. I was the better looking, better dressed, better employed and was even driving a better car. I was leaving all of that aside, because we had such an energetic and engaging conversation online and again in person. I was letting the half-truths and the dirty car slide, and I wanted a second date. But the dumpy slob had the nerve to say our age difference was the "elephant in the room." I took the high road and did not respond in a mean-spirited manner. What I really wanted to say was, "You were panicked because I am way outta your league. Why don't you clean all the fast food trash out of your car before you ask someone to ride with you." This person was much taller than me and that was the main attraction for me. I did not mind the size or age difference up until that point. But I felt I was and still am a "catch." You must feel the same, but as I learned, just because you perceive yourself one way, does not mean others feel the same about you, your looks, your financial resources or your taste.

Often a younger person expects an older person to have their life more together, their finances, and their home, even the cleanliness of their car. But a person who is older or younger than you is no more likely to have their life in a better situation than yours. If the older person is intimidated on a date with a more successful, or more attractive younger person, they may try to use the age difference as an excuse to not go further.

Age differences must be a topic openly discussed and both parties must feel comfortable. Your comfort can also not be limited to private meetings. If you want to develop a relationship, you must feel comfortable introducing your much older or much younger mate to friends and family. You both must be prepared for a backlash. The greater the age difference, the more other people will feel it is their business to comment on your May-December romance. You both must feel contented and happy in your relationship to be able to weather the intrusion of the thoughts and opinions of other people.

The reasons that one dates a different age group than their own are as varied as people themselves. The wisdom and self-assuredness that comes from maturity can certainly be a huge draw to a younger person. Tolerance and independence of spirit are very attractive as well. Some people seek a mentor as well as a partner. Maybe you just don't want children and dating a person who is beyond that child-rearing age is attractive.

Avoid limiting yourself to a particular age range. If child bearing is of vital importance to you, be aware that your older man may not be as active and you may need to do more of the work. If you happen to fall for a younger man and you are past childbearing age, there are thousands of children in the adoption systems that are desperate for two loving parents. If you fall for an older man and want to raise children, the mechanics are easier, but he must be prepared to take little Johnnie or Joanna to baseball or softball practice, just like his younger counterparts.

As long as you both are in agreement that your attraction is mutual and you love each other, then dating a person of a different age is something to be celebrated. If your family are not supportive, then you must make it clear to them that this person is important to you. If you truly feel a connection, your family will have to accept him, or they will not have as much time with you.

As I said before, be prepared to laugh off the comments about your age difference. My friend Joe's mother says: "Better a babysitter, than a nurse." Or "I'd rather push a stroller than a wheelchair." Come up with your own comebacks, and be ready!

Chapter 18
Dating a Married Person/Dating While Married

While I do not recommend it, some people like to date the married folks. There is a certain comfort in this type of arrangement. Those who fear commitment will often who follow this path. Once in a while it just happens that you fall in love with a person who is technically unavailable. Sometimes you are the married one and you are exploring other outlets for intimacy. This intimacy can be as innocent as a cup of coffee and talking about your thought, fears and accomplishments.

If you must go in this direction, be discrete and respectful of the non-involved partner. Remember that you are taking time away from the spouse and possibly their children. If you are the married one, remember that your spouse and children have a vested interest in how you spend your time.

My own father had two part-time companions as he moved through life as a married man. He also had numerous one-time affairs. This is still common in many cultures and was common in the U.S. until the late 20th Century. Many people feel it is wrong, but I try not to say what is wrong or right for others. I said *try*. It is preferable to see what works best for you. For my father, it was normal to have other women in addition to my mother, and later, my stepmother. It was common knowledge and was rather an open secret that he had other women in his life. On various occasions, my next older brother and I spent weekends with one of my father's girlfriends, to give he and his wife some time alone. While such relationships are no longer common in the US, I do believe that every couple is entitled to set their own rules, so long as they are not harming anyone. I know that there are wives who feel that it is their right to explore other sexual options when their husband is away on business – or when they have to travel for work themselves. This is sort of a Don't Ask, Don't Tell policy. Generally this is not dating, but simply one-time sexual encounters.

I do not recommend extra-marital affairs, but I am also not one to judge what is a personal matter for those involved. At the same time, I am against doing anything that will harm your relationship or your partner (even as I speak from guilt). There is a strong community of free love couples worldwide. They are called "swingers" and generally are married couples that enjoy switching partners with other secure married couples. Usually this is not dating, but only sexual encounters. On some occasions, one couple will date another couple. This has been going on for thousands of years, just as men have frequented brothels for thousands of years. It is not going away, regardless of how much the US culture would like to deny its existence.

You may not want to participate, but for those who consent to be part of this community, there is nothing wrong in it. Let me be clear, I only advocate consensual behavior. I do not promote sneaking around and doing things behind the back of the person you are dating or have married. Dating must always be an open dialog. Let your partner know if you feel a need to roam and perhaps they will understand. Or possibly they will partake in some role-playing or the dialogue will lead to other exploration of different aspects of your relationship. Maybe the two of you will invest in some costumes or take a weekend away to stay in a hotel, so that you can role-play or simply get out of your normal routine.

Chapter 19
Arguments

Surviving the first full-blown argument is a huge step in a relationship. It means that the person you have chosen has also chosen you, and is not running away at the first sign of trouble.

As for the actual argument: It was your fault. Let me repeat, it was your fault.

That is the first thing you have to know. But you do not ever have to admit. Admitting that the cause was your doing is a decision you have to make on your own. As far as your partner in life will be concerned though, it was YOUR fault and always will be. That's fine if you know this fact going in.

Allow him to always think that he is right. But secretly you may know that you are right at least 75% of the time. You may want to even agree to disagree sometimes, just to let it go.

Let me be clear here about fighting that I mean arguing. I do not mean knock-down, drag-out, hitting, punching fights. Unless you are professional boxers, professional street fighters or professional wrestlers, DO NOT HIT. If someone hits you, even if it is the person you are dating or want to marry, CALL THE POLICE. Assault is still assault if it comes from someone you love. Never fail to recognize this.

So back to fighting fair... The best way to fight fair is to not bring up anything that happened more than one month back. If in doubt, don't bring it up (well that is unless you have not already covered it in a previous argument.) Bringing up anything over a month old sort of violates the statute of limitations on things.

If you can bring up something that occurred two years back, then inevitably something five years old can be brought up. Once you go that far, why not bring up things that occurred before you even met one another. It's not healthy and not productive. Speak up with what is hurting you now. Tell him what he did TO YOU – or how he made YOU feel. Something that he did can seem perfectly harmless to him, but for you, it can be devastating.

What was the intention behind a particular action? Was your man intentionally trying to hurt you? If he was, that is another matter. But when the argument is about something that was never intended to harm, you must understand that point in the course of the argument. You must keep in mind that it is the action that has you upset, more so than the man you are dating. It is behavior and it can be corrected.

In his book, "The Mathematics of Divorce," John Gottmen discovered that when you have a classic stonewalling husband and a wife who criticizes often, that is not a basis for divorce. Many marriages go on for 70 plus years with this type of exchange. What Gottman discovered is that the most important factor in divorce is *contempt*. It sounds so simple. The problem is when the disagreements cross the line into feeling *contempt* for the other partner. Merriam-Webster defines contempt as an intense feeling of disrespect and dislike. It is related to feelings of resentment and bitterness. Having these feelings in the intense moments of an argument are not grounds for a divorce. It is when these feelings are present long after the argument has settled and the partners are still unhappy and unsatisfied.

In my own family, if you had the chance to ask my father's mother about her relationship, she would never have used that word – but the concept is the same in all the years of their marriage – through the alcoholism, the financial losses during the Great Depression, the triumphs and tragedies. They survived as the classic criticizing wife and stonewalling husband. In later years, he would turn off his hearing aid when he needed quiet. Never did the contempt for one another that one feels in the heat of an argument grow to a point where it existed in the peacetime of everyday life. Neither felt superior towards the other. This is really the basis for contempt – feeling superior to the other and thus beyond criticism. Of course there are times when one feels superior to the person one is dating, or even the one you married. But at a certain point, when it becomes the predominant feeling or reaction, then the relationship is likely to end soon, unless acted upon by some other force.

This carries through in the case of a partner's sexual history, money issues, etiquette, and the like. When one partner feels superior in too many areas of life or, conversely, when one partner continually feels inferior – it weighs heavily on the relationship. If you begin a relationship with a very wealthy person and you are not wealthy, you may feel intimidated. If you are a wealthy person and you are with a person who barely had two nickels, you may feel superior to your partner in that area. In order for the relationship to last and thrive, you must work to find the areas where one excels and the other is lacking. Find the things that balance your relationship. One may be rolling in money and the other may bring looks, manners, taste, education or some other factor. One may have the looks and one may have the hot body. One may be the smart one and one may be the moneymaker. As I have said and will continue to say in this book, things in a successful, thriving relationship need NOT be <u>completely</u> balanced. There must be a give and take. If you look up "balance" in the dictionary, you will see "equilibrium" and "stability" – two things that are your dating and relationship goal, even in the heat of an argument.

Do not pry into private information. If you suspect your man of unfaithfulness, it does not give you the right to start reading your man's email. Do not listen to his voicemail messages. No not hack into his online profile.

Invading the other person's privacy is a violation not only your man's trust, but also the trust he has with anyone who left those voice messages and emails. If you feel that you are being betrayed, ask him, ask others around them. If he is not being unfaithful and you have violated his trust and that of his friends, it will be hard for any of them to trust you in the future.

On the flip side, do not lie. Something that seems like a small lie to save your man's feelings, can blow up into an issue of mistrust. Try your best to always tell the truth, even when it may hurt. This will allow you to be trusted (by your man and others).

Chapter 20
Dating and Sexuality;
It All Comes Down To Shagging

Recently I was talking about sex with several women in preparation for this book. One of the women spoke up and asked me how she could tell if her boyfriend is gay or bisexual. Surprised by the question, I asked her what she meant.

She said that her boyfriend loves super heroes. He reads comic books and has costumes of several super heroes that he wears on occasion (not just at Halloween). Okay.. and???

Well she came out of the shower one day and he was sitting on the floor of her apartment mending his Spiderman costume. She thought that this meant he was gay or something.

After about thirty to forty-five minutes of discussion about their sex life and interests, it came down to this: Her boyfriend has a superhero fetish, plain and simple. He likes dressing up in spandex and wanted to "rescue" his girlfriend.

My advice was simple. Get to a costume store as soon as possible and buy a Catwoman costume. I instructed her to surprise her man by dressing up one night and playing out the superhero fantasy with her man.

Results were wonderful.

For many people, it is tough to raise the discussion of when to take the next step in intimacy. Discuss your feelings directly, if you can. You may want to use language that is delicate or even euphemistic, if the subject is too uncomfortable. There was a professional wrestler some years back who used the term "pie" to refer to sex and also to a woman's vagina. This pie reference made for some very funny speeches in the ring. You can use this type of reference to be direct or vague, but the conversation must be had at a certain point, if you feel ready to take a relationship to the next level. Ask him if he likes pie, several times, with a wink and a nod. If he responds correctly, you have solved the delicate issue. You need to be clear that you are both on the same page, even if you have to actually ask some questions. One has to be sure not to offend, or seem too eager. You must also discuss, or at least mention, safer sex practices.

When asked about dating and sex, one of my closest friends says: No sex for at least 2 months. I feel that this is long, but you have to decide what works between you in your unique relationship.

Sexual activity is a natural part of life, and the interaction between people. Sex, in and of itself, is neither good nor bad (contrary to popular belief). As a woman, sexual activity is much more likely to be tied to emotions. This is part of the human female genetic makeup. Most other animals have no problem engaging in sexual activity and then moving right along. Many people function the same way and assign no connection between sexual activity and love. Being able to keep sex separate from love is not a bad thing. But you need to know where you fall in this spectrum and also be able to gauge where the other person stands as well. Most people in the US attach emotions to any sexual activity these days, so be prepared for the possibility of entanglement.

What we are discussing here is the process after one has established a rapport, and seeks to consummate a dating relationship. There is no greater intimacy then sex. Sharing your body, blemishes and belly fat, breasts and cellulite, nipples and lips – is the most refreshing and intimate expression of caring that can be given. When you know that the time is coming to consummate your relationship, be prepared to look your best.

For men and woman, this can mean grooming the private parts. In recent years, for men, this has been jokingly referred to as Manscaping. This includes trimming the area of importance, so that all things are accessible. Woman may not know that rolling up a hair in a condom can be a painful experience. Also recall that body hair often holds in odors. Do not go overboard with the trimming, but make things neat. You get a haircut on your head, so that you look sharp and put together, your private regions can be groomed in the same manner.

Bathing is important and making sure that all things are clean and smelling fresh, makes for a much more pleasant experience. This is particularly true if your paramour is a man who likes to begin with oral attention to your private areas.

Men should not expect to receive oral attention, unless they are prepared to offer the same. Women are much more likely to be multi-orgasmic than men.

Very often, they can go and go. So if he wants to please you, he must be taught to not only warm you up with foreplay, but to give you that attention he expects in return.

Women, please be aware that most men can be turned on very easily and would love to skip directly to intercourse. Take them on a journey to get there, and they will appreciate the ride. Some men take more time to get things together, and can be easily turned off if a woman is too aggressive with her needs. First and foremost, sexual activity is a balancing of the two egos involved. Both of you may already have emotional or psychological baggage in your head, from previous sexual experiences and relationships.

This is where my earlier suggestion to discuss things beforehand comes into play. Some people have very sensitive nipples, and for them, this is the "on" button. Others have a very sensitive neck, tummy, inner thigh, etc. If you can jokingly, or in a whisper, ask this kind of information before, you may have a better time, and create a better experience for your man. If he is a little evasive in conversation – that means he wants you to explore the whole body; and discover those arousal areas for yourself. Remember that the buttocks and anus are extremely sensitive on both men and women, much like the nipples, the vagina and the penis. It does not make him gay just because he wants to give attention to your behind. Nor does it make him gay if you want to do the same to him.

Whatever you love doing, ease into it gently and see how he responds. Start kissing on the back of the neck, and work your way all the way down. You and he will be amazed at how many nerve endings there are, and how erotic it can be for you. There are many sensitive areas on the human body. Try biting him on the hips, the shoulders or the back of the knee. Explore, explore, explore.

I know of some people who get sexually aroused from receiving a foot massage and others who get arousal from giving a foot massage. This kind of symbiosis can lead to a very erotic sexual exploration of each other.

AROUSAL

Many adults need to be in some form of an altered mind-set to reach orgasm. Let me explain what I mean: Arousal is very often triggered by factors that are considered fetishes. But most people don't think of their interests as a "fetish." What I am discussing are the trigger items that get you or your man aroused. This can be as simple as eye color, hair color and as complex as role-playing clothes like a French maid or sexy kitten costume.

A small percentage of these adults use drugs (both legal and illegal) to reach this altered state. I do not encourage the use of anything illegal, but the altered mind-state can often be achieved with mild hypnosis or reaching a low-level trance. You may have experienced this and not recognized it was happening. Conversely, you may have bewitched a man into doing things with you that he did not expect. Something as simple as a fetish for high heels, can entrance a man to do your will. There are many triggers for achieving this heightened arousal, or altered mindset.

For some men, the race of the woman is a big factor. Breast size is a very common bewitching factor. It may be the Big Buxom Woman (BBW) who hypnotizes a man, without any effort on her part. For others it is the rail-skinny body type that not only attracts, but creates that altered mind-set or eroticism. Women are just as likely to have these trance-like trigger factors. The actual triggers will vary in an infinite number of directions. For some people, this daze-like state of arousal can be created by their partner using a soft voice and intimate, but directive words. Some women will be caught in a spell of sorts by the flexing of a man's bicep, others will feel it when they see the man take the lead to protect her in a crowd. When you discover a man's trigger points, you can use them to guide him into making you happy, all the while making him happy as well.

If your man's trigger point is the curve of a woman's neck, be sure to wear clothing that shows off your long neck. Ask him to put on your necklaces for you, so he can kiss your neck as he does so. If he likes the calves, make sure you show yours off and cross your legs in a way that shows them off so he can see them. He will be drawn even further and faster.

Many people have hang ups about their sexuality, or about their bodies. Most Americans feel that they are too fat. If you are full figured, remember that the person you have been dating already knows your size. Clearly, they like you, and your full figure. Do not let your body-image issues keep you from enjoying a fulfilling sexual experience with a person who likes you. Use it to bewitch him into falling head over heels in love.

If the man you are with is not doing what he needs to do in order to have you at full arousal, then you may guide him gently. Without complaining that he is too rough or not focusing on the right area, you can gently redirect his face or hand to the right place. Whisper instructions to him like "to the left" or "a little higher". If he is going to fast, don't complain and ruin the mood: simply whisper, "ok, now slower." With some gentle coaxing and encouragement, your new man can be guided into becoming the lover you want.

If you have children – their presence is a factor. If the sex turns out to be good, and your kids and families do not get along - dating may not work long term. If the families get along and the sex is bad - this may be a chance to teach or learn, so you can grow together; or it may be your opportunity to end the dating and find someone else.

In summery, if you have been dating and feel this man is worth going to the next level, have the discussion and see how it goes. If the all goes well, you will explore and enjoy. This may be the mid step toward your future happy marriage.

Chapter 21
Victory

Once you have figured out what you want and have a candidate for dating, look beyond your common interests and see that they are ready for a relationship of the level you seek. People tend to think of levels of compatibility based on the number of activities or hobbies they can both enjoy together. Sometimes this is just a default mechanism people use when asked to describe what they are looking for in a mate.

Common interests have the ability to bring two people together, but do not carry enough weight to make a relationship successful. You may start with a shared passion for golf or sailing and together you grow from there. But a relationship should not be based solely on one or two common interests. It is very helpful to have one or two hobbies you can enjoy together—but this should not be the end all, be all. Sometimes the dating process starts with one shared interest and then the couple find it is hard to get off that track, so it's very important for people to realize that an activity is just one part of the picture, not the main focus.

This comes back to the idea of finding a person who shares your values. If you met through a hiking group, you are both more likely to be outdoor people and may share similar interests other than hiking. This can mean that you also share a common set of values: conservation, concern for the environment, recycling or even botany. However, if you met during the intermission at a play, you may have been drawn to the theater from completely opposite sides.

One may be there solely for the story and the other because they love the theater company producing the work. Sharing one interest helps introduce you to others, but then you must delve further and learn whether their value system matches and compliments your own.

Does your date value work over family, do they attend church, are they agnostic, do they recycle and do they want or already have children? Are they close to their parents and/or siblings? What do their friends think of them? What would their enemies say about them? These are questions you need to think about as you decide for yourself what counts in your dating life, as you move toward a permanent relationship. As the answers become clearer, so will your answer to the question, "Is this the person for me?"

Identify the person or type of person that best fits you, based on personality and values. I am not saying go for the Brad Pitt look-alike because of his looks. You need to identify what key values run through you and your beliefs. You may value the type of person who puts family before anything, and then you may encounter a single dad who works as a mechanic. He may not even be on your radar, but his values may fit better than anyone you have met in your forty years. Be open to it. You may have your sites set on a model like Taye Diggs or athlete like David Beckham. But then you may meet an executive from a competitor company and he just knocks your socks off. You don't even notice that he is five years older than you and then within months, his daughter's soccer games become the highlight of your weekend. It happens. Be ready.

Once you have found the one, what do you do now?

Here the real work begins as you manage the complexities of in-laws, blended families and even maintaining passion. You can do it. You have learned to love yourself and be open to the love of another. You have learned to put the toothpaste away for the 400th time and recognized that sometimes it's just easier to not sweat the little things and focus on the love you have welcomed into your life.

Some last points to go over before I let you go:

I recommend against living together before marriage. Studies have shown that people who do a "test drive" before marriage are actually less likely to stay together once they get married. There are exceptions, and this is something you and your man must decide.

Do not rush into marriage, even if the person you have found seems to satisfy everything you hoped they would. Research has shown that the majority of people need to date around two years, before committing to the bond of marriage. Remember, it's not just the one person you are marrying. You are bringing them into your family, and you are becoming part of theirs. When in-laws or children do not get along, it can wear on a marriage and the couple at the center of the storm. Again, every situation is different; I am just giving a statistic as a guide.

Have a discussion about really big issues before you get married. How will you handle your finances? How many children do you both want? It is important to clarify these questions before the honeymoon. Premarital education or counseling can help with this. Studies also show that those who go through this process have higher levels of marital satisfaction and are more committed to their spouses. If you do not want children, it can be a huge problem if your spouse wants five of them. And if you are a financial mess, you need to discuss this beforehand. You may want to surrender the money management to the one with better skills in that area.

Arguments can be bitter and horrible sometimes. Learn to avoid: non-constructive criticism, contempt, defensiveness, and stonewalling. Learn to tone down heated arguments with humor and a few kind words. You have a vested interest in this relationship working. If you can make him laugh in the middle of an argument, then you are leaps and bounds closer to a resolution.

Often, men want to think they are taking care of you. Despite the fact that many women are outpacing men on the college level and in the workplace, lots of guys still derive their feelings of masculinity and self-worth by being of value to the person they love. If you are the independent type who can support herself, step back at times and let him step up -- even if it's just to do something as simple as pay for dinner. I used to know a woman who could change a tire and do minor repairs to cars. I was grateful that she showed me how to do some things. But to some men, this would be intimidating. If you feel that working on your own car will intimidate him, find something else that he can do for you, to replace that sense of caring after you. Think of it this way: Letting him care for you shows you care for him.

Take time for intimacy even when it seems like you don't have a minute to spare. Remember that 30 seconds of holding the man you love can help see you through an entire day of hardship.

Take time to give each other compliments and remember to say "please" and "thank you" rather than barking orders or nagging. Even the simple task of closing the toilet seat lid or making breakfast needs to be addressed and appreciated. Making the bed or taking out the trash are worthy of a hug and a thank you.

Choose the right partner. This one decision will determine 90% of your happiness *or misery*.

How is wealth really measured? Ask yourself!

May you always have love to share, health to spare and friends that care.

Thanks for reading!

Acknowledgements

My thanks to Lee and Anna Wilson for sharing stories of their journey to love. Thanks to Lee and Joni Norton, to Clint J. Allen, Suzette Clair, Dylan Page, Lolin Martins-Crane, Karyn Plonsky, Ty Davis and Winston Batchelor for each allowing me to include their stories, suggestions and gossip about their other friends.

Special thanks to Brevard N. Hudson for being my editor, sounding board and guide.

◄ <u>References – Further Reading</u> ►

Neuro-Linguistic Programming, Richard Bandler and John Grinder Neuro-Linguistic Programming (NLP) is a collection of pseudoscientific self-help rituals proposed for programming the mind.

The Pocket Guide to Becoming a Superstar In Your Field, Spitfire Communications. 2006.

Layered Neural Pyramids, Jeff Dahms, http://www.nyu.edu/classes/neimark/jeff.html

First Impression Management , http://www.fim-inc.com

The Meaning of Color for Gender, by Natalia Khouw http://www.colormatters.com

"The Mathematics of Divorce," by John Gottmen

◄ End Notes ►

[i] By: Marjabelle Young Stewart, Ann Buchwald, Charles Moll • Publisher: New York, D. McKay Co. [1969]
[ii] Neuro-Linguistic Programming, Richard Bandler and John Grinder Neuro-Linguistic Programming (NLP) are a collection of pseudoscientific self-help rituals proposed for programming the mind.
[iii] Dating for Dummies, by Joyce Browne, (1997) page 116.
[iv] By: Blaise C. Hancock, used with permission (2009)